breakfast

recipes to wake up for

breakfast

GEORGE WELD & EVAN HANCZOR *of* Egg

photography *by*
BRYAN GARDNER

RIZZOLI
NEW YORK

contents

Every person who's walked through the doors at Egg in the past 10 years— whether it was to work or to eat or to deliver food from the farm or just to say hello—has had a hand in making this book. Thank you all.

foreword

Barely 10 years ago, George Weld, a schoolmate from Charleston we hadn't seen since graduation, came to us for advice. He planned to open a restaurant in Williamsburg, Brooklyn, he said, serving real Southern breakfast: grits and eggs, biscuits, country ham. We weren't quite sure why he'd come to us. Our own Southern-in-the-Big-City notion—selling boiled peanuts—had been a total failure, and we'd beat a hasty retreat to Charleston, morphed the peanut impulse into a mail-order catalogue, and were shuttling up and down I-95 trying to keep that business and our fledgling freelance-writing careers afloat.

We admired George's pluck, especially when he told us that his culinary chops were self-taught, and he'd never worked in—much less owned—a serious restaurant. But seriously: a *breakfast* place? In *New York*? We'd spent enough time in the city to know that bitter coffee and a cold, buttered bagel from a street-corner cart passed for breakfast in the Big Apple. We had one word of advice: *Don't*.

Fortunately for him and for New Yorkers, he ignored us. A half-dozen years before *pop-up* would become de rigueur in the start-up lexicon, George arranged for a burger-and-dog joint on North 5th Street to share their tiny kitchen and dining room during the morning hours, from 5:00 a.m. until noon. At the crack of dawn, "Sparky's" became "Egg," and you'd see him hauling produce boxes in the door from a battered Subaru. Later that morning, he'd be sweating through his trucker's cap and T-shirt, but skippering his kitchen with a laser-like focus on the transcendence of simple, everyday indulgences: a slice of brioche perfectly crisped on the griddle and spread with fig jam. A buttery, tender omelet. A French press of strong coffee. Real cream. The atmosphere was no-frills—folding chairs, drawing paper, and cups of crayons on the tables, but oh so warm, with sunshine streaming through the south-facing windows and the young waitstaff introducing customers to the pleasures of sorghum and pimento cheese.

You wanted to linger there, which soon became difficult as the *New York Times*, *New York*, and *Time Out* wrote rapturous reviews, and lines for tables became common, even on weekdays. Egg was an overnight success: for the neighborhood it became a daily habit, but it was special enough to inspire destination breakfasts, too. After a couple years, Egg assumed Sparky's lease and served breakfast all day. Egg became a community, and George's kitchen a holding pen for top Brooklyn talent between bigger gigs; chefs who did time in Egg's kitchen ended up opening their own places or helming the kitchens of a village of restaurants: the Commodore, Roebling Tea Room, Saltie— all neighborhood anchors known for their straightforward comforts, exacting technique, and outstanding value. The Odeons and the Balthazars of the boroughs.

Breakfast is the beautiful distillation of Egg's 10 years of making people happy in the morning. George is precisely the person to learn breakfast from—it was his patient, deft instruction that taught us to perfect the rolled omelets that have made us heroes in our households. *Breakfast*'s simple, elegant indulgences—lemon cornmeal cake, candied bacon, smoked bluefish hash—could fire up the impulse toward *real* breakfast in the most shot-of-espresso-and-out-the-door kind of soul. Already an early-morning stove jockey? Excellent! This book will add new fields (savory oatmeal, confit) to your morning game.

So wake the hell up! And get cooking!

—MATT LEE & TED LEE

in defense of morning

Breakfast is both the most moralized and most debased of all meals. Everyone knows it's important, but most people treat it with all the enthusiasm of balancing a checkbook. This meal is so compromised that some of the most heavily processed foods we eat all day are considered the healthy option at breakfast. Try making Rice Krispies or Wheaties on your own and you'll quickly get a sense of what sort of industrial apparatus is necessary to concoct those seemingly straightforward staples of the table.

People throw out all kind of excuses to avoid eating actual food at breakfast. Many people eat breakfast alone and don't want to make something that requires time or thought or, God forbid, washing a dish. Or they're feeding children who won't eat anything more interesting than pepperoni pizza even when they're rested and alert, to say nothing of when they're groggy and angry about having to go to school. Or they don't like waking up, and the thought of cooking before they're over their general anger at being out of bed feels like too much to overcome.

At Egg, we've heard all those objections and then some, and we're here to tell you that there's a better way. When we opened in 2005, most people thought the very idea of a breakfast restaurant in New York was absurd—especially in Williamsburg, a neighborhood more famous for all-nighters than early risers. No one in New York had time to sit down for breakfast, we were told. But we stuck it out. I felt pretty sure that once people had given it a shot, they'd be converted. I knew we could convince them to give up their energy bars and street-cart bagels and sit down to wholesome meals of properly cooked eggs, organic grits, vegetables we'd grown, and sausage we'd made. And soon enough, even in this neighborhood of night owls, people were waiting outside the gate for us to open at 7:00 a.m.

If foggy-headed musicians and exhausted film editors will haul themselves out of bed on an icy New York City morning for pancakes and scrambled eggs, you can too. Just put your feet on the floor and stand up. Stagger to the kitchen and make coffee. You've done the hard part. Great breakfast is a habit you can adopt with less effort than you think—most of the dishes in this book are made from pantry staples and require nothing more exotic than maple syrup and black pepper. You just need to shift your focus a little. Think about making your mornings memorable, not dreadful. Instead of letting dinner drive your thinking, put your imagination into making something that will put you on course for a good day. In the process—by thinking about breakfast first—you can get the rest of your week's meals lined up almost effortlessly.

Many of the recipes in this book are so simple you can make them in minutes; some are longer and more involved, the kind of thing you might spend a couple hours preparing on a Sunday that will yield a week's worth of delicious, instant morning meals. And when you commit to taking breakfast seriously, you'll find your dinners will improve almost automatically. Once you've mastered egg cookery and added country ham to your pantry, you can turn a mundane bowl of mixed greens into a showpiece salad. Or take one of the slow braises we recommend for breakfast and serve it for dinner without any adjustment at all.

Being able to cook a good breakfast will make any home cook a hero to family members and houseguests. Your co-workers will wonder why you come to work alert and content, deaf to the siren song of the cellophane-wrapped donuts in the office vending machine. If you master the skills to cook great breakfasts, you'll cook better at every other meal, and you'll make better use of your time in the kitchen than you'll ever do as long as cereal retains top billing on your breakfast menu.

This book is both a plea and a guide for making the most of your mornings, for transforming the breakfast industry-bestowed tagline—"the most important meal of the day"—into something we take seriously. I've never met a person who's made a habit of waking up early who says it's not a better way to live. Breakfast is, for many families, the only time everyone is awake and gathered together under one roof. It's when many people are at their most productive and intelligent—their minds are focused, uncluttered by the noise of the day. In 10 years of serving breakfast at Egg, we've seen remarkable things happen to people as they lingered over breakfast—they've fallen in love, started businesses, written books and songs. We've watched parents spend precious quiet time with their children, sharing pancakes as they brace each other for a day of school and work. It happens every day: people come in a little groggy and dull; they leave awake and alert and well fed. Get up, get cooking, and let breakfast transform your life.

—GEORGE WELD

in the kitchen

The breakfast pantry is easy: It's almost all stuff you're likely to have on hand anyway. The basics are good eggs, whole butter, whole milk, flour, baking powder, salt, and pepper. You can make a feast with nothing more than that. And frankly, we recommend keeping things as simple as possible. Who wants to start their morning worrying about whether they've got the right spice blend to make a recipe work? We rely on a few seasonings for almost every purpose at Egg—salt and black pepper, red pepper flakes, turbinado sugar, apple cider vinegar.

But when you're keeping things simple, it's especially important to get the best you can. I remind anyone who balks at paying a premium for food of this simple truth: You are putting it in your body. It is in fact *becoming* your body. If there's one area of your life NOT to skimp on, good food is surely it.

APPLE CIDER VINEGAR

Making food taste good is a matter of balancing elements—fundamentally, saltiness, sweetness, spiciness, and acidity. After saltiness, acidity is the most important of these for making a dish come to life, and apple cider vinegar is our go-to ingredient for brightening up a dish. We use it in everything from our sausage to our biscuits, where we use it to sour milk (a trick we learned from the undisputed master of our craft, Edna Lewis).

Choose a good-quality vinegar: If it tastes good enough to drink (just a bit!), then it's good enough. We get organic unfiltered vinegar from Spectrum that still has the flavor of apples.

BACON FAT

In the house I grew up in there was always a can of bacon fat on the back of the stove. I keep my bacon fat in the fridge now, but I use it fearlessly, whether I'm sautéing onions for a sauce or searing a steak. It's delicious, and it's far more economical and sustainable to use bacon fat rendered from a pig who lived nearby than to pay for olive oil imported from halfway around the world. So save your bacon fat! When you cook a pan of bacon, just pour the fat from the pan into a ramekin or other heat-resistant container and put it in the fridge.

BLACK PEPPER

Black pepper is so ubiquitous it's almost impossible to imagine being excited by it. But really good peppercorns are remarkable. When you first crack them they smell incredibly complex: floral, bitter, spicy. If your peppercorns have languished in your pantry for years, consider replacing them. We like to get ours from a fair-trade certified source. Get some fresh ones, crack them into your palm, and give them a gentle whiff. If you've been taking pepper for granted, you'll be amazed anew.

BUTTER

Butter's gotten a bad rap over the years. You probably shouldn't eat it by the spoonful, but there's no reason to entirely deny yourself the pleasures of good butter. We use unsalted butter in all the recipes in this book. If you have good bread to toast in the morning, slathering it with fresh butter from a grass-fed cow and a little sea salt can be all the breakfast you need.

CAST-IRON SKILLET

A 10- or 12-inch cast-iron skillet should just be part of your daily cooking. Cast-iron skillets hold heat well, cook food evenly and efficiently, and last forever. (Actually, they get better the more you use them.) If you haven't inherited one, go get one now and use it as much as you can—for cornbread, for frying, for cooking potatoes.

CHEESE

We serve just one kind of cheese at the restaurant—a sharp aged cheddar from Grafton Village Cheese in Vermont. We like sharp cheddar for breakfast because it stands up well to eggs and grits, which is how we usually eat it. But almost any cheese can be a great addition to breakfast, from a pillowy triple cream to a ripe blue. If you want a quick, wholesome, and delicious breakfast, a slice of cheese with a little bread and jam gets you well on the way.

CHEF'S KNIFE

You don't need an extensive selection of knives to make breakfast, but you should have one good chef's knife. Get something good enough that you'll be inspired to take care of. Buy a honing steel, and use it frequently. Then just keep your knife from banging around in the bottom of the sink or rattling around in the dishwasher or a silverware drawer, and you'll have a tool that makes dicing onions a joy.

CLARIFIED BUTTER

We cook all of our eggs (except scrambled) in clarified butter. It's good for all manner of sautéing and searing. Using clarified butter instead of whole butter is a cleaner way to cook eggs—there are no milk solids to brown or burn in the pan, so the eggs come out nice and white.

It can be a bit of a pain to clarify small amounts of it. If you want to use clarified butter, buy 4 or 5 pounds of butter and clarify it all at once. (At the restaurant, we clarify butter 20 pounds at a time.) Put the butter in a sturdy pot over low heat to melt it. After it melts, it will start to separate: first a foam will rise to the top, which you can skim off with a spoon. Second, the solids in the butter will start to fall out and drop to the bottom of the pot, leaving a clear golden liquid behind: That's the clarified butter. Carefully pour it out of the pot, leaving the settled milk solids behind. Store it in the refrigerator and just scoop out what you need for a dish with a spoon. It keeps indefinitely.

EGGS

For us, it all begins with eggs. They've been called nature's perfect food and they've been vilified as the nutritional equivalent of a pack of cigarettes. They have the most ignominious beginnings of almost any food, but from the moment they hit the nest they're the very symbol of culinary charm and beauty. They're simple, portable, versatile, and delicious.

Eggs are among the easiest foods to buy directly from a farmer. In rural areas you'll often see them for sale out of someone's house, a little sign in the driveway to lure you in for a dozen still-warm eggs. If you can't buy them like that, look for local eggs at your farmer's market or grocery store. Chickens who've been able to eat outside lay eggs that taste, cook, and nourish better than chickens who don't get out.

If you can get your hands on duck eggs, as we do when our ducks are cooperating, try substituting them for chicken eggs in pancakes: they'll make the lightest pancakes you ever had. They scramble nicely, too, though they can be so rich they're almost overwhelming.

And if you have a backyard, give a thought to raising your own chickens. It's not hard and even a couple of chickens will give you almost as many eggs as you can eat. They're surprisingly personable and funny, too—I've come out of the house in the spring to find ours snuggled up with my children in the hammock.

FLOUR

We use several different types of flour in our kitchen at Egg: a high-gluten unbleached wheat flour; a bleached all-purpose variety; and pastry flour, which has the lowest gluten (and, frankly, nutritional) content of them all. For almost everything we cook, we use the unbleached flour, which is milled from wheat grown in New York State. We reserve the bleached and pastry flours for biscuits, which need low-gluten flour to keep them light and crumbly.

GRITS

We have a lot to say about grits in the Grains chapter, but here's what to look for when you're buying them: stone-ground grits that need to be refrigerated. Quick grits that sit on the shelf at the grocery store year-round are tolerable as vehicles for lots of cheese and gravy, but if you want to eat the real thing, seek them out from a purveyor like Anson Mills.

HONEY

A single bee can make about a gram of honey in the course of its life, so when you look at a pint of honey you're looking at the life's work of 500 to 600 bees. How's that for teamwork? You can get honey at any grocery store, but we strongly recommend finding a local source at a farmer's market. In New York, our purveyors offer honeys in a wide range of colors and flavors—they're harvested at different points in the season to correspond with the peak blooms of different flowers: linden, Russian olive, lavender, clover. We can even get honey harvested from rooftop hives in the city itself. The flavor difference between different types of honey is striking and worth exploring.

MAPLE SYRUP

Growing up in the South, I got maple syrup once a year, when my grandmother had some sent to us for Christmas. The rest of the year we mostly survived on Aunt Jemima or Mrs. Butterworth's.

In New York, maple syrup grows on trees. In the woods near our farm in the Catskills you can see webs of plastic tubing connecting maple trees to vats that collect sap. That sap is only faintly sweet—it's much closer to water than to syrup. To turn it into the elixir we pour over pancakes, it's slowly reduced over low heat for hours and hours—reduced so far, in fact, that 10 gallons of sap yields only a quart of syrup.

We use Grade B syrup in the restaurant—it's richer than the lighter Grade A (though no cheaper). Keep a quart in your fridge for your pancakes and you'll find you want it on your ice cream, on an almond butter sandwich, or in a bowl of plain yogurt. It makes an especially good sweetener for coffee—some cold brew with whole milk and maple syrup is our favorite way to get caffeinated.

MILK

We get all of our milk at Egg from Ronnybrook Farm Dairy, a third-generation family farm just a couple of hours away from Brooklyn. Their milk is unhomogenized and sweet, not subjected to the ultra-high-heat pasteurization of commodity milk. Seek out a local dairy to patronize if you can, or buy milk from a local farm at your grocery store.

MEAT

You've heard it a thousand times by now, but we'll say it again: Be careful about how you buy your meat. Modern industrial meat production is a disaster from every point of view—economically, ecologically, gastronomically. That's true even if you don't value the life of animals; if you care about how animals are raised and slaughtered then you have a whole other host of concerns.

But animals raised for meat on a small scale can be an important part of creating a sustainable food system: on a small farm, where animals are raised on pasture or locally produced grains, where grazing is worked into a rotation with vegetable or grain production, animals fulfill an important part of the nutrient cycle, converting grasses and grains into fertilizer that lays a foundation for healthy vegetables and fruit.

We buy all of our meat from farmers who are committed to the humane treatment of their animals and careful stewardship of the land. Many of them are local to our area, but we also buy a lot of meat through Heritage Foods USA, which buys meat from small farms all over the country, including places where there's no local market for pasture-raised meats. You can buy from them, too—they deliver nationwide.

MOLASSES

Molasses was the syrup of first resort in the house I grew up in, so it's been a surprise to me to learn that not everyone likes it. Dark, heavy, and a tiny bit bitter, it's incredible poured over cornbread or buttered biscuits. It's a valuable addition to a pot of collards, too, but our favorite way to use it is in a milkshake—two scoops of vanilla ice cream covered by just enough milk to bathe it, and a tablespoon or two of molasses. And why shouldn't you have a milkshake for breakfast?

NONSTICK PAN

You don't need much specialized equipment for cooking breakfast at home, but one pan we consider indispensable is a nonstick pan just for your eggs. You can make do with cast-iron or even steel, but you'll suffer a lot of frustration trying to flip your eggs out of a heavy pan. We use 8-inch pans for every kind of egg except omelets, which we cook in a 10-inch pan. If you're careful not to scratch them and you don't leave them sitting over a blazing hot burner, you'll get years of use out of a good nonstick pan.

RED PEPPER FLAKES

When we need a little extra spice—to liven up a rich gravy or heavy stew, for instance—red pepper flakes give us an easy way to do it. There are more interesting ways to make something spicy, but red pepper flakes are durable, versatile, and easy to work with before you've had your coffee.

SALT

Salting your food properly is one of the most important skills you can develop as a cook. When it's done right, salting enlivens the flavor of everything. If you taste a dish and it seems flat or bland, start by adding a little salt. You'll be amazed how often the flavors of a dish will spring into relief just with the help of salt.

We use kosher salt because it's easy to work with. You can grab a good quantity easily in your fingers, and you can see it as it lands on the food you're seasoning, which makes it easier to tell whether you've added enough. Sometimes when we're feeling fancy or when we want to feel the crunch of salt between our teeth we'll add a little coarse sea salt, like Maldon, to a dish just before we serve it.

SUGAR

We use turbinado sugar more than any other sugar—unlike refined white sugar, turbinado retains some of the molasses flavor from the cane, which makes it more interesting. We do use standard white sugar in a few recipes—pound cake, which needs the texture of white sugar to cream properly; and fig jam, which doesn't want the extra richness that turbinado sugar provides—and maple sugar on special occasions. But just about everything else, from biscuits to coffee, we use turbinado.

VANILLA

Vanilla is another of those pantry staples so common that it's almost invisible. Chances are you have a bottle or two of uncertain vintage and provenance in your cabinet right now. But think about this: Vanilla beans are the fruit of an orchid. They're as exotic and as beautiful as flamingos.

I once read in an esteemed cooking magazine that there was no discernible difference between real vanilla and imitation vanilla. That's not true: The difference is stark. Buy real vanilla, the best that you can, and the next people to eat your pancakes will thank you.

YOGURT

We use a plain, unstrained, whole-milk yogurt from Ronnybrook Farm Dairy. It's tangy and refreshing, thick enough to hold up a pile of granola but not the paste-thick "Greek-style" yogurt that's swept the market these days—we'd rather use that to glue up wallpaper. When we need a slightly thicker version—as in our recipe for roasted carrots and yogurt—we'll pour it into cheesecloth and strain it for half an hour or so.

eggs

If you learn to cook eggs properly, you will be a better human being. They're miraculous foods: nutritious, versatile, good at every meal. They deserve—and they reward—our respect and attention.

The key to cooking eggs is being gentle—gentle hands, gentle heat. Resist the urge to cook them in a sputtering pan, which will cause them to blister and brown. Eggs are the only protein I know of that doesn't benefit from browning—high heat just makes them tough without improving their flavor at all.

Every cook who comes to work at Egg arrives sure he knows how to make eggs. And every cook gets retrained, because almost everyone learns eggs wrong. You can always tell a cook who won't last by the way he reacts to being shown how to cook eggs properly. If you can't be thoughtful and humble in front of a simple egg, you're never going to be able to cook well.

scrambled

serves 2

A well-made scrambled egg is a miracle of transformation. It is simple in the extreme, but it's even simpler to screw it up beyond repair.

What we go for when we scramble eggs are curds that are just set—not still runny or raw, but not tight and jiggly. There's a brief period between the time they're still oozing in the pan and the moment they become tight wads of hopelessness. Turning them out on the plate while they're still in the former zone is your goal.

A few basics. Aside from a pan, a spatula, and heat, you need three things to make good scrambled eggs: good eggs, salt, and whole butter. Don't mess with any of the improvements you may have read about over the years—cream, milk, cream cheese. Learn to make eggs without those crutches. Salt your eggs as you cook them (there's an old myth that says you shouldn't salt eggs until you're done with them, but it's only a myth). Serve them as quickly as possible after you finish them—they'll only get worse as they sit.

2 tsp unsalted butter

4 eggs, cracked into a bowl

kosher salt

Heat an 8-inch nonstick pan over medium heat. When the pan is hot enough to melt butter but not hot enough to brown it, add the butter. Add the 4 eggs and a pinch of salt before the butter is fully melted—you want some of the water from the butter to mix in with your egg to help inflate them with steam. Poke the eggs with a spatula to break the yolk before the whites begin to set. If the whites begin to set immediately on hitting the pan, remove the pan from heat. Stir the eggs with a silicone or wooden spatula and mix until the eggs are uniformly blended.

Keep an eye on the eggs, stirring them as they begin to set around the edges. Be especially vigilant once the eggs have nearly all set: When you see only traces of liquid egg on the bottom of the pan as you stir, remove the pan from heat, stir the eggs one more time, and turn them out onto a plate to serve immediately.

You don't need to stir constantly to get good eggs. Stir them enough to keep them from setting too hard in any one place. If they start to set, break them up. Then you can leave them alone until they seem ready to set again. Turn them out of the pan when they're just still glossy and wet—they'll cook another degree or two off heat.

PRO TIP

If you want to add cheese to your scrambled eggs, add shredded cheese just before they finish cooking. If you add the cheese too early, the eggs won't set properly and you'll end up with a gloppy mess.

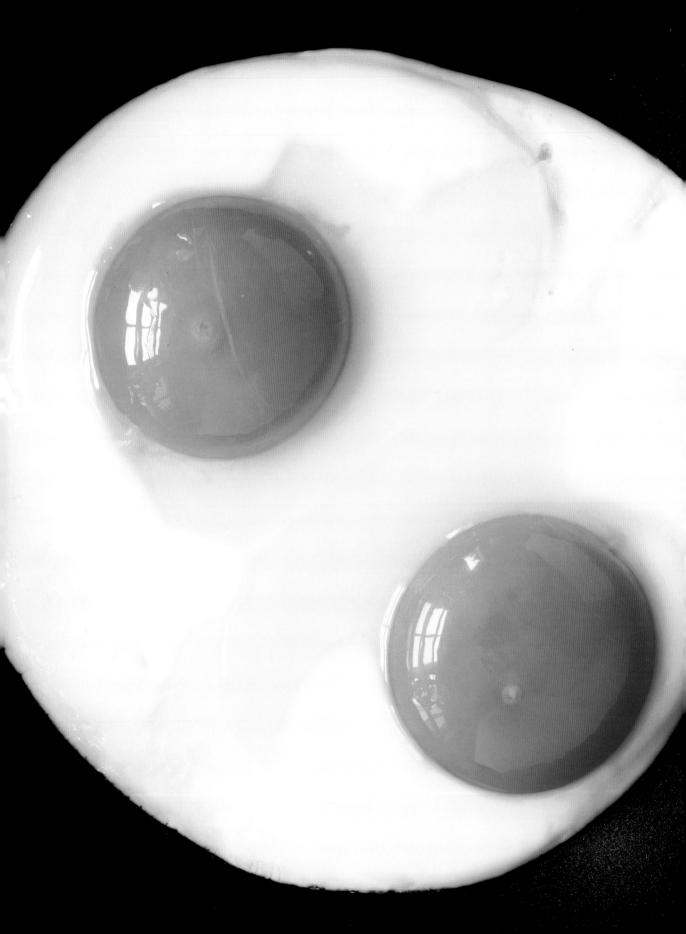

over-easy (-medium, -hard)

Every new cook in Egg's kitchen gets nervous about her first order of over-easies. The pressure is on and the risk of failure is high. The skills this dish requires—a sensitive touch, a quick hand—are a metaphor for everything that matters in breakfast cookery. There's not much to know, but if you don't get the little movements just right, you end up with badly scrambled eggs rather than perfect over-easies.

serves 1

2 eggs

1 tsp clarified butter or vegetable oil

kosher salt

black pepper

Crack 2 eggs into a shallow dish. If you get a bit of shell in the dish, use a spoon or fork to scrape it out (it's a lot easier than using your finger).

Heat a teaspoon of clarified butter or vegetable oil in a nonstick pan over medium heat. Slip the eggs into the pan gently. If they sizzle, turn the heat down immediately or remove the pan from heat. You want the whites to set gently in the heat, not fry and sputter.

Once the outer white is fully set and remaining white just set (as shown in photo opposite), gently shake the pan to make sure the eggs are loose from the bottom. Jiggle and shake the pan until the 2 yolks are in a line at right angles to the handle of the pan (if the pan is a face and the yolks are the eyes, the handle should be the neck).

Now comes the fun part. To flip eggs, you'll move your hand in a rapid, vertical circle, like a Ferris wheel. You're not really trying to launch the eggs out of the pan so much as guiding them up into the air and then catching them gently as they descend back toward the earth. Make your moves confident and quick. Holding the pan in the air, push the pan away from you in a slight downward arc, like you're passing through the bottom of a loop-de-loop. As the pan starts to come up again from its low point in the loop, give it the slightest flick, as though you're just letting the eggs know it's okay for them to take flight. This flick is also what sets the eggs into rotation so that they come down on the raw side.

>>

Your hand should be moving back toward your body now, completing the top of the loop. Catch the eggs on the downside of the loop as they complete their flip while you lower the pan again.

Assuming you've successfully flipped your eggs without breaking the yolk, put the pan back on heat and let it cook for 20–30 seconds, or until the inner white immediately around the yolk looks set (it's hard to see from the bottom, but gently touch the egg just next to the yolk—if the white is still runny, you'll be able to tell).

When the inner white has set, you can either slip the eggs out onto a plate straightaway or, if you're feeling confident, flip them a second time back onto their pretty side. Sprinkle with salt and black pepper.

PRO TIP

Everyone breaks eggs sometimes. Sometimes it's the egg's fault, not yours. But you can increase your chances of success by practicing, and once you get it you'll be set for life. If you don't want to waste a couple dozen eggs trying it, put a slice of bread in a pan and practice flipping that. You'll get the basic motion down that way, and then you'll just have to work on the details.

poached

serves 2

2 fresh eggs in poaching, the fresher the better

2 tsp apple cider vinegar

1 quart water

kosher salt

black pepper

It was a poached egg that brought me back into the fold of egg-eaters. I'd been burned by too many bad eggs growing up: sulfurous scrambleds, gray-rimmed hard boileds, and chalky poached eggs. One day, I made a poached egg just for the challenge of it. I sprinkled some kosher salt and ground some black pepper on it, took a piece of toast out of the oven, and sat down to a tiny meal that changed the way I felt about eggs. As I cut into it, I watched the yolk surge out onto the white plate, and sponged it up with a piece of bread. This was all I ever wanted in food: sensual but simple, the dumb rapture of falling in love.

People often tell you to poach your eggs in a deep pot. We don't bother with that; we poach eggs in a shallow 1 quart pot. Some also say you need to swirl the water in your pot gently to create a vortex to drop your egg into. We don't bother with that, either. It makes a good mess of your pot and doesn't really improve the shape of the egg.

People are split on whether to add vinegar to the water and how much to add. We always do, partly because we like the flavor a touch of good vinegar adds, and partly because it makes the eggs easier to handle. (Eggs poached without vinegar are wildly slippery, which is fine for home, but pretty hard to handle when you're trying to carry five plates of food out to the dining room without losing anything.)

Crack the eggs into two individual cups. Bring 1 quart of water to a boil over high heat, then reduce to a high simmer. Add vinegar. Lower the edge of the cup to just above the surface of the water and slip the egg in.

Let the eggs set for a few seconds before taking the edge of a slotted spoon and scraping it across the bottom of the pot to make sure the eggs didn't stick. If they're floating free, just let them cook gently in a simmering pot for 3 minutes.

Remove the eggs one at a time with a slotted spoon, being careful to let all the water drain back into the pot. Check the egg for doneness: You should be able to see a well-formed orb of liquid yolk set into a gently-set disk of white. (Sometimes the inner white won't set fully and it will make the center of the egg look a little bulbous— if that's the way your egg looks, just slide it back into the water for a 20–30 seconds.)

Once your eggs are done, slide each one onto a plate and pull away any unsightly scraps with your fingers. If any water puddles around the egg, you can either pour it off or sop it up with a paper towel. Sprinkle with salt and pepper.

sunnyside-up

serves 2

2 tsp clarified butter or vegetable oil

2 large eggs

Sunnysides are pretty simple: just lay some eggs down easy into hot butter and cook them gently. But simple as they are, they require some finesse. Because they're so simple, it's tempting to try to rush them. But the fact is that they're the slowest eggs you'll cook in a pan. If the heat is too high, you'll brown the edges and make the outer white tough before the inner white has even begun to set.

Don't salt sunnyside eggs until you're ready to eat them—the salt will pucker and discolor the yolks!

Pour a little oil or clarified butter into a nonstick pan and heat over medium-low heat. Crack 2 eggs into a bowl and inspect for bits of shell and leaking yolks. If everything is okay, slide the eggs into the pan.

If the eggs sizzle immediately when they hit the pan, remove them from the heat right away and reduce the flame or the temperature on your burner. You don't want the edges of the eggs spitting and fluttering in the heat.

Cook eggs slowly until the tops of the whites are set and yolk is still runny, about 5 minutes.

omelet with stewed summer beans (page 162)
and simple roasted potatoes (page 149)

omelet

If you've never had anything but American diner omelets, this variation will open your eyes. This delicate, tender preparation shows off the eggs so well that we don't put anything inside except a little sharp cheese.

You can certainly add other ingredients if you like, but take some time practicing this basic recipe first. It's a little tricky, but well worth mastering. It works by constant movement to keep the curds of the eggs small and moist, so that you end up setting a thin, supple sheet of just-set eggs in the bottom of the pan before you roll the omelet out onto a plate.

makes 1

3 large eggs

1/2 tsp kosher salt

1 tsp clarified butter or vegetable oil

1/4 cup (1 oz) sharp cheddar cheese, shredded

Crack eggs into a small bowl, add salt, and stir vigorously with a fork to homogenize the yolks and whites. Beat the eggs until you can't see the difference between yolks and whites any longer—they should be completely mixed together. If the eggs still look clumpy when you lift the fork through them, keep mixing.

Heat butter or oil in a 10-inch nonstick skillet over medium-high heat. When the pan is hot but not smoking, pour all the eggs in at once and start stirring with the back of your fork.

As you shake the pan and stir the eggs, you're helping to keep the eggs from setting up large curds. The goal is to get a thin, supple, delicate sheet of egg to set across the bottom of the pan at the very moment the eggs on the exposed (upward-facing) side are cooked enough to eat but not a bit more. You'll achieve this by moving the pan and the fork constantly as the eggs set.

After 30 seconds or so, the eggs will be mostly set: they'll be opaque and smooth against the bottom of the pan and wet and loose on the exposed surface. At this point, pull the pan away from heat and use the back of the fork to smooth and spread the wet parts of the eggs out into any gaps to create a single solid layer of just-cooked eggs in the bottom of the pan. Add the shredded cheese.

>>

Now it's time to roll the omelet: Off heat, reverse your grip on the pan handle so that the line of the handle runs from the pan past your pinky and exits your hand on the thumb side. As you grip the pan, your fingertips and first knuckles should be facing you.

Holding the pan facing you, lower it so that the bottom edge is just above the plate you want to serve the omelet from. Starting at the top edge of the pan, use your fork to roll the eggs over in a tight roll, like you're rolling up a dollar bill. It's key to get the first roll of the eggs tight— it'll help give the finished omelet a good shape.

Roll the eggs down the pan, tightening up the roll with your fork as you go, until the eggs roll out onto your plate. They should look like a big yellow cigar. If you homogenized the eggs properly, there should be no streaks of white, and if you set them properly in the pan they should have a smooth, delicate outer skin. You can tidy up the roll with your fingers once it gets on the plate.

boiled

serves 1

2 eggs, ends pricked with a thumbtack

The only time slightly older eggs are preferable to fresh ones is when you boil them. Fresh eggs are much harder to peel than older ones. Our eggs are all very fresh and tend to be hard to peel so we use a trick to make the peeling easier: We poke a thumbtack into the end of each egg before we boil it. I can't say for sure why that helps, but it seems to.

For proper hard-boiled eggs, use the smallest pot you have that will hold the number of eggs you're cooking plus just enough water to cover them. It's critical to get them to the boil as fast as possible.

Put your eggs in a 1 quart pot with just enough water to cover them. Quickly bring to a boil over high heat. As soon as the water boils, gently stir the eggs once and take them off heat (stirring helps keep the yolk from settling on one side of the egg).

Leave the eggs in the hot water and start a timer. The times you want are:

Soft-boiled: 3 minutes
Medium-boiled: 6 minutes
Hard-boiled: 10 minutes

As soon as the timer goes off, dump out the eggs and rinse with cold water (if you're making hard-boiled eggs, plunge them into an ice bath). Serve soft- and medium-boiled eggs in egg cups with toast, if you like—just cut off the tops of the eggs so that you can eat them right out of the shell.

With hard-boiled eggs, you can either peel them right away (it's easiest to peel them while they're still in the ice bath before they're completely cooled), or you can store them in their shells for 5 days.

pickled

These are classic beet-pickled eggs—
they come out vivid fuchsia. Sliced
open, so that the dark yellow yolk is
exposed, they're one of the prettiest
foods you can put on a plate.

yields 6 eggs

1 red beet

olive oil

kosher salt

black pepper

6 hard-boiled eggs, peeled page 31

1 clove garlic, gently smashed

2 cups apple cider vinegar

1 cup water

Preheat oven or toaster oven to 350°F. Rub the beet with olive oil, salt, and pepper. Place in a sheet of aluminum foil, add a splash of water, and wrap tightly. Roast for 40–70 minutes (the timing depends on the size of the beet), until it's tender enough that a fork slides easily to the center of the beet.

Remove the beet from the oven and let cool. When it's cool enough to handle, rub or cut the skin off (this'll be messy, so consider where you work and wear rubber gloves if you have them).

Cut the beet into chunks and put into a jar with the hard-boiled eggs. Add the smashed garlic and pour the cider vinegar and water over top. The liquid will quickly turn purple, and within a day the eggs will have picked up the color and flavor of the pickling liquid.

Serve with salt for a snack, or sliced in a salad or on toast.

deviled eggs with country ham (page 100)

deviled

Deviled eggs are standard picnic and hors d'oeuvres fare, but they're just as suitable for breakfast. You can make a fine morning meal from a couple of deviled eggs, some slices of country ham, a biscuit and jam, and some pickles or stewed vegetables.

makes 12 pieces

6 hard-boiled eggs, peeled page 31

1/2 cup mayonnaise

1 1/2 tsp prepared whole-grain mustard

1 tsp pickled jalapeños, minced

1 tsp sandwich pickles, minced

1 tsp pickled red onion, minced page 177

1/2 tsp juice from the jalapeño pickle jar

Slice each hard-boiled egg in half longwise and remove the yolk into a bowl with the back of your thumb or a small spoon. Be careful not to tear the white. Set the whites aside.

To make the filling, use the back of a wooden spoon to press the cooked yolks through a sieve into a bowl. Add mayonnaise, mustard, pickled jalapeños, sandwich pickles, pickled red onion, and jalapeño pickle juice to the bowl and stir until everything is well blended. Taste and adjust based on your desire for salt, spiciness, and crunch. Using a teaspoon or demitasse spoon, fill each white with a generous amount of deviled yolk.

eggs rothko

serves 1

1 1-inch thick slice of brioche, challah or any soft, rich bread

2 tsp unsalted butter or olive oil

1 egg

1/4–1/3 cup aged cheddar cheese, shredded

This is our most popular dish at Egg. It's a version of a pretty classic dish that goes by many other names— egg-in-a-nest and toad-in-the-hole are the ones we hear most frequently. Ours got its name from a friend who was helping us get Egg open. Mark Rothko was her great-uncle, and— as I recall—family lore held that this was his go-to breakfast.

This dish begins with good ingredients (a good fat slice of bread; a sharp, aged cheddar cheese) and ends with a careful pass under the broiler. The only tricky thing to it is to get the egg set just enough that the whites aren't runny but not so much that the yolk is cooked. We serve ours with a dollop of broiled tomatoes, but you could achieve the same effect with a few shots of hot sauce or any other brightly flavored relish. It's nice to have something to cut the richness of the dish.

Preheat your broiler.

Heat a broiler-proof pan on the stovetop just big enough to hold your slice of bread over medium heat.

Use a 2-inch biscuit cutter to cut a hole out of the middle of your bread (use a knife if you don't have the biscuit cutter, but make sure the hole's not too big).

Place the bread in the heated skillet and put the butter or olive oil into the hole. Crack the egg into a dish (make sure the yolk stays intact). Once the butter has melted, slip the egg carefully into the hole in the bread.

Let the egg cook over medium heat until the white around the bottom has set. Don't wait for all the white to set—you just want to make sure it's set on the bottom and sealed to the bread, about 3 minutes. Using a spatula, carefully pick up the bread and egg and turn it onto its other side (make it quick but be gentle—you don't want to break the egg).

Immediately spread the shredded cheddar evenly over the top of the bread, making sure to take it to the edges (it'll keep the bread from burning in the broiler). Cook for 45 seconds, then slide the entire pan under the broiler to melt the cheese.

Rothkos will hold a few minutes without suffering, so if you need to make several, just put the cooked Rothkos somewhere warm to hold until you're ready to serve them all.

hash

People tend to think of hashes as potato-based dishes, and many of them are. But traditionally, at least in the South, hashes are fundamentally about thrift and economy—about transforming a few scraps of food into a meal for a family. Gravy-based hashes, poured over biscuits, are part of the repertoire. I learned that from an uncle one morning as I stood in the kitchen at my grandmother's farm, trying to figure out what to make the family for breakfast the day after Thanksgiving. "Make a turkey hash," he said. "But we don't have any potatoes," I complained. And so he taught me what to do.

We love both gravy- and potato-based hashes at Egg. We sell a lot of biscuits and gravy, but we also love building hashes on a foundation of grated russet potatoes fried crisp on the griddle. In fact we love hashes so much we started a food cart called Hash Bar just to showcase them. We serve hashes with everything from pimento cheese to duck confit to snap peas to braised goat. We've included a few favorites to get you started, but let your imagination roam. Once you've got the basics down, you can make a king's breakfast out of a few remnants.

hash browns

serves 6

4 medium (2 lb) russet potatoes
or other high-starch/low-moisture potato

1/4 cup onion, minced

kosher salt

black pepper

oil for deep frying

These hash browns were inspired by a thousand disappointing home fries. Once in a great while, I've found a restaurant that served properly cooked home fries for breakfast, cooked through to tender and crispy on the outside. But most of the time you get a plate of mealy, soft-edged potatoes, pallid onions clinging to them like wet leaves. With enough ketchup or a debilitating-enough hangover you might find them edible, but as a rule they are disgusting.

And it's a shame, because a well-fried potato is one of life's great pleasures. Why it's not considered acceptable to eat French fries at breakfast is a mystery, but these hash browns are better than fries anyway. They make home fries seem lazy and lame.

They're not terribly easy to make. Cooking them is a two-step process: They have to be peeled and grated by hand and hand-formed before they're deep-fried. But if you're cooking for a crowd, or you happen to have a deep fryer, you can turn a humble spud into a showstopper.

Put the potatoes in a deep pot and add cold water to cover. Bring to a boil over high heat, then turn off flame and let the potatoes sit in the boiled water for 8 minutes.

After 8 minutes, confirm that the potatoes are cooked by poking them with a knife—they should receive the tip of a knife easily, but without getting smushy (if they're smushy, it's too late for hash browns. Drain them and make mashed potatoes or soup). Pour the potatoes out into a colander and let them dry.

While they are still warm, peel the skin off each potato (you may find this easier to do with a paring knife than with a vegetable peeler, which can get gummed up).

Grate the potatoes into a bowl on the coarse side of a box grater. You can also grate them using the grater attachment of a stand mixer, but don't grate them in your food processor—they'll turn to goop.

Mix the minced onion into the grated potatoes, then season generously with salt and pepper. Mix well with your hands.

While the potatoes are still warm, scoop them up a handful at a time, about 1/2 cup, and form them into oblong disks with your hands. Pack them by bringing your hands together around the grated potato as though you were clapping. You want them tight. You may find you have an easier time of it if you dip your hands in clean water between each hash brown.

Once the hash browns are formed, you can wrap them tightly in plastic wrap and store them overnight in your fridge. If the potatoes are properly cooked, the hash browns won't turn gray. Even if they do, they'll still taste good. At this point, you can use these for any of the potato-based hashes in this book.

To cook, use a fryer or fill a pot at least 2 inches deep with oil. Heat oil to 350°F and fry the hash browns in batches small enough that they don't crowd. Each one should take about 5–7 minutes. Once they're cooked, hold them on a drain rack or a few layers of paper towel until you're ready to serve.

flat-top hash browns

serves 4

Crispy potatoes and melted sharp cheddar cheese: There are few combinations more delicious. We start by smashing individual hash browns onto a hot griddle with a little oil or clarified butter to help them brown. These become the foundation for most of our potato-based hashes.

2 tbsp bacon fat, unsalted butter, or olive oil

4 hash browns, formed and unfried page 40

1 cup sharp cheddar, grated

In a large skillet or griddle, heat a tablespoon of the bacon fat, butter, or some vegetable oil over medium high heat. When the oil is hot enough to sizzle when you touch a bit of potato to it, smash the hash browns down on the oiled griddle. Spread grated cheese on top of each section of potato.

Let the potato cook undisturbed for 5–7 minutes, lifting up an edge from time to time with a spatula to see if the potato is browning.

Cook until the underside of the potato is golden brown and the edges are crisp, then fold each hash in half so that it looks like a taco with the cheese tucked inside.

biscuits & gravy

Biscuits and gravy isn't pretty, but it can get your day off to a great start. It's as comforting as a crackling wood stove and a lot easier to eat. We've been surprised to find that this dish sells especially well on the hottest days of summer. (This is a good use for day-old biscuits; just make sure you reheat them thoroughly before using.)

serves 2

2 biscuits page 72

2–4 fresh sausage patties or 1–2 large links; about 2–4 oz altogether

1 tsp flour

2 cups milk

kosher salt

black pepper

cayenne pepper

Put your biscuits in a warm oven or toaster oven to heat through. If you're using link sausage, slice the links open longwise and discard the casings.

Heat a small or medium stainless steel sauté pan over medium-high heat. (Do not use a nonstick pan for this recipe.) When the pan is hot (you can test it with a small piece of sausage—it should sizzle right away), add the sausage all at once. Use a wooden spatula or spoon to mash the sausage down on the pan while breaking it up into chunks (or bite-size pieces). You want to brown the sausage and get a little of it to stick to the pan to create what fancier cooks call a "fond."

When the sausage is nicely browned (but not necessarily cooked through), about 5 minutes, you should see three things: well-browned chunks of sausage, a nicely browned residue on the bottom of the pan, and some rendered fat. (If there's not much rendered fat, you can add a little vegetable oil or bacon fat.) Sprinkle the flour into the pan, stirring it into the fat. Cook the flour in the rendered fat and sausage for a minute, turning down the heat if necessary to keep the flour and pan residue from burning.

Pour milk into the pan, being careful not to splash. Use the end of the spatula to scrape the residue from the bottom of the pan, then stir the cooked flour, the deglazed fond, and the sausage together. Bring the gravy to a boil, lower the heat, and let it cook until it thickens, about 8 minutes. When it's ready, gravy will be the thickness of heavy cream.

Split your biscuits and arrange in shallow bowls. Taste the gravy and add salt, ground black pepper, and cayenne to taste. Pour over the biscuits and serve immediately.

vegetarian gravy

This makes a good version of biscuits and gravy for folks who don't eat meat. Just make sure you check for seasoning: since mushrooms aren't as inherently spicy as sausage, you may need to add a considerable amount of salt and pepper to the gravy to make it savory enough.

serves 2

1 tbsp + 1 tsp vegetable oil, divided

1 1/2 cups cremini mushrooms, chopped
about 8 medium size, cut into odd-shaped wedges to keep them interesting

kosher salt

black pepper

1 tsp flour

2 cups whole milk

cayenne pepper

Heat 1 tablespoon of vegetable oil over medium-high heat in a steel or cast-iron pan until it is hot enough that when you put a mushroom in it, it sizzles immediately. Add all of the mushrooms to the pan and stir so they are all coated with oil. Sprinkle with salt and a grind or two of black pepper and allow to cook undisturbed until they are well-browned on one side, about 3 minutes. Then turn to cook further on the other side.

Turn down the heat to medium and sprinkle the flour into the pan, stirring it into the hot vegetable oil. If necessary, add remaining teaspoon of oil. Cook the flour in the oil and mushrooms for a minute until the flour begins to color slightly.

Pour milk into the pan, being careful not to splash or spill. Use the end of the spatula to scrape up any residue from the bottom of the pan (if there is any), then stir to blend the cooked flour and the mushrooms together. Bring the gravy to a boil and lower the heat and let it cook at a slow simmer, stirring occasionally until it thickens, about 8 minutes.

When it's ready, gravy will be the thickness of heavy cream. To serve, pour over hot biscuits and season with more pepper, salt, and cayenne pepper to taste.

duck hash

serves 4

Ducks are incredibly delicious and versatile birds. Duck breast is as delicious as steak and easier to cook. The thighs and legs are delicious braised or as confit. Duck eggs are deliciously rich on their own and do an incredible job filling in for chicken eggs in pancakes or cakes.

   This dish—an easy variant of our basic hash recipe—uses just a smidgen of duck confit, but it's as hearty and rich as a much bigger meal. Use a little of the duck fat from the confit pot to cook the potatoes for best results.

   We've included only the most basic vegetables for this recipe, the ones we include in it no matter the season. But try adding sliced ramps in the spring, kernels of corn in the fall, or top with some sour cherry compote in the summer.

1 cup duck confit, shredded page 132

1 tbsp duck fat, bacon fat, or olive oil

4 hash browns, formed and unfried page 40

1/2 carrot, finely diced

1 rib celery, sliced across the stalk into 1/8-inch pieces

6 scallions or spring onions, thinly sliced

Allow the confit to warm up enough to get it out of the fat. Set aside some of the fat to cook the hash browns in.

In a large skillet or griddle, heat a tablespoon of the duck fat (or bacon fat or some vegetable oil) over medium high heat. Smash the hash browns down on the oiled griddle (as described in the flat-top hash recipe on page 42).

Scatter the carrot and celery pieces by the side of each hash brown so that they can cook in the fat coming off the potatoes. Add scallions and cook for 2–3 minutes, until the carrot and celery start to soften, and then divide the duck evenly into four piles on top of the diced vegetables.

Once the duck is warmed through and crispy on the very edges, tuck it and the vegetables into the hash browns and fold the hash browns in half so that the duck and vegetable are inside. Transfer to plates and serve alone, with a salad, or some eggs and pickled ramps (page 169).

smoked bluefish hash

serves 4

1 small bulb fennel, with some fronds for garnish

1 tbsp + 1 tsp olive oil

3/4 cup snap or snow peas, trimmed and cut cross-wise

kosher salt

1 lemon

4 hash browns, formed and unfried page 40

1 cup smoked or grilled bluefish, flaked into bite-size pieces

If you've ever gone fishing, you know the value of getting up early. My uncle used to wake me at 4:00 a.m. on summer mornings to catch bait fish before we headed a few miles offshore to troll for king mackerel and bluefish. The water was smoother than glass as the sun rose, and we'd often find ourselves escorted by a pod of dolphins. You can skip the predawn fishing trip and sneak some fish onto the grill the night before you want to make your hash. At the restaurant, we use bluefish because it's available and sustainable, but this dish will do fine with any white fish.

Trim and halve the fennel bulb, then cut out the core. Cut the bulb crosswise into thin slices about the width of a match.

Heat a teaspoon of oil in a sauté pan to very hot and toss in the peas and fennel slices. Cook until peas are bright green and just seared and fennel is aromatic and softened. Season with a sprinkling of salt and a dash of lemon juice. Pull off heat and set aside

In a larger skillet or griddle, heat a tablespoon of oil over medium-high heat. Smash the hash browns down on the oiled griddle (as described in the flat-top hash recipe on page 42). Spread a quarter of the fish over half of each hash brown. When the potatoes are browned and crispy on the bottom, distribute the peas and fennel among the four hashes before gently folding them in half and transferring to a plate. Garnish with fennel fronds and a slice of lemon.

red flannel hash

serves 4

Most of Egg's culinary cues come from the South, but there are some Northern dishes we love, and this is at the top of the list. A hearty, easy-to-prepare hash of corned beef, marinated beets, roasted potatoes, and bitter greens, it's a great way to start a winter morning.

1 tbsp vegetable oil

2 cups roasted potatoes page 149

2 cups corned beef, cubed page 123

2 cups marinated beets page 172

2 cups bitter greens, chopped

Heat a large sauté pan over medium-high heat. Add oil and toss in the roasted potatoes just long enough for them to get crispy again. Add the corned beef and beets and toss. Once the beef is warm, add the bitter greens and toss again. Cook until the greens are just wilted. Remove from heat and either serve right away, or hold in a 325º F oven while you cook some eggs.

red flannel hash with poached egg (page 25)

spring vegetable hash

Hashes aren't just for heavy meats.
They make a good backdrop for
vegetables, too.

serves 4

1 bunch broccoli rabe around 6 stalks

4–6 radishes

1 tbsp unsalted butter

kosher salt

black pepper

1 tbsp + 2 tsp oil

1/2 tsp lemon juice optional

4 hash browns

1/4 cup hard or semi-hard cheese, grated cheddar or aged gouda

6 spring onions or scallions, chopped

Trim off any dry or woody ends of the broccoli rabe and split the stalks into pencil-thick pieces if they're thick. Trim the greens off the radishes and cut them into quarters or sixths.

In a small sauté pan, heat the butter over medium heat until it's foaming. Add the radishes and sauté until they're browned at the edges and tender. Remove from the butter and season with salt and pepper.

Wipe out the sauté pan and heat a teaspoon of oil over medium-high heat. Add the broccoli rabe and some salt, pepper, and lemon juice to taste. When the stalks are tender and the florets lightly seared, remove from heat and set aside while you cook the potatoes.

In a larger skillet or griddle, heat a tablespoon of oil over medium-high heat. Smash the hash browns down on the oiled griddle (as described in the flat-top hash recipe on page 42). When the potatoes are browned and crispy on the bottom, divide the cheese among the pieces and allow to melt for a minute before adding the vegetables. Lay the broccoli rabe and radish on half of the hash browns. Scatter the scallions throughout the pan, allowing some to sear on the surface and some to stay more or less raw on top of the potatoes. When the cheese is melted, fold each hash in half and transfer to a plate with a spatula. Serve with eggs or a salad or on its own.

grains

Growing up I developed the idea that each part of the country had its own special morning grain: up north they ate oatmeal; in the Midwest they ate cream of wheat. Out west it was rice with beans. And where I grew up, in the South, it was grits.

I hated grits. In our house they were instant and flavorless and I didn't see any point in eating them. I would let them sit on my plate as I picked at the rest of my food, watching as cold spread up them like spring coming to the mountains, congealed first around the foot, and then up the slopes to where a pat of butter sat melting in a pool on top. Fully congealed, they were suitable for reenacting some lesson from earth science class—modeling the lava flows from Mt. St. Helen, for example. I'd cut a channel in the edge of the butter's crater and watch it flow down the slopes to the plate. The games made it easier to withstand the silent approbation of my mother for leaving them on the plate. And if I could withstand that long enough, it was possible to get out of eating the grits altogether.

Grits were redeemed for me after college when a friend of mine in New York served me a plate of stone-ground grits he'd ordered from our mutual friends Matt and Ted Lee. The Lees had just started a little provisioning company to keep expatriate Southerners stocked with grits and boiled peanuts, and Chris had a bag of their grits, ground at a North Carolina mill. We sat down to eat, fully in the grips of nostalgia: Emmylou Harris on the stereo, the Lees' catalogue—a hand-stitched booklet printed on brown grocery-bag paper—on the table beside us, and fish and beans and grits for dinner. Eating those grits was a watershed moment for me. They had substance and color and the delicate, summery flavor of corn. I was converted. It was one of the first hints I got at the richness of Southern culinary traditions that I grew up experiencing mostly in bastardized and sterilized forms.

There's something beautifully simple about eating grains for breakfast: a bowl of steel-cut oats, still recognizable as the seed of a plant; a plate of fresh-milled grits, redolent of corn—these don't need much fuss to feel like the right thing to eat first thing on a cool morning. You can take last night's leftover rice and heat it up up with vegetables for a quick dirty rice or toast a mix of oats, nuts, and seeds for homemade granola.

grits

Grits are good all day, every day. It's worth keeping a supply of cooked grits in your fridge for daily consumption. Cook a batch two or three times a week when you have time to fuss over a pot for a bit. When you're hungry, reheat them with a glug of cream or a dollop of butter, throw in cheese if you like, or cover them with a stew or a quick sauté of vegetables and eggs, and you've got a nearly instant breakfast that's worthy of the most decadent weekend meal.

1 cup stone-ground grits

3 cups cold water

1 tsp kosher salt

1 tbsp unsalted butter or 2 tbsp heavy cream

Combine the grits and water in a pot. Stir grits vigorously so that chaff floats to the top of the pot. Skim off with a small strainer.

At this point, you can either cook the grits immediately or leave them to soak overnight: soaking reduces the cooking time by almost half, so if you anticipate being pressed for time, consider soaking.

To cook the grits, put the pot over medium-high heat and stir frequently, making sure you get to the bottom of the pot as you do.

When the grits reach a simmer and begin to thicken, reduce the heat to lowest setting and cover. Stir after 5 minutes, then every 10–15 minutes and check for sticking. Cook until grits are tender—about 90 minutes for unsoaked grits—adding water each time you stir, up to 1 additional cup.

Just before serving stir in butter or heavy cream.

CHEESE GRITS

To make cheese grits, take a regular batch of hot grits and add a sharp, semi-hard grated cheese to them shortly before serving. We use an aged cheddar from Vermont, but they're good with aged gruyère—and with pimento cheese, too. Let your tongue tell you just how much cheese to add, but count on about 1/4 cup per serving.

winter squash grits

serves 4

This is a simple and delicious dish, excellent for breakfast but equally good as a side at dinner. There's something intellectually pleasant about combining corn and squash in this way, as they grow together so famously well. They taste great together, too.

3 cups cooked grits page 56

2 tbsp cream or unsalted butter

boiling water

1 cup sage-roasted squash page 155

kosher salt

black pepper

3 leaves fresh sage, julienned

Put the grits and the cream or butter in a small pot with about 1/2 cup of boiling water to loosen them up. Warm them over medium-low heat, stirring constantly. Add more water, a little at a time, until the grits are just liquid enough to stir easily. Add the squash and use a wooden spoon or fork to mash it into the grits. Continue heating until the grits are hot throughout and the squash is dispersed into the grits, turning them a beautiful orange. Taste and adjust for salt.

Serve with fresh cracked pepper and a little fresh sage.

winter squash grits with sautéed kale (page 140)

simple oatmeal

serves 2–4

Good steel-cut oatmeal is easy to cook. It takes a little time, but it's well worth it. Steel-cut (or cracked) oats are so much more interesting and delicious than the paste you get from cooking quick rolled oats.

1 cup steel-cut oats

1/2 tsp kosher salt

4 cups water

turbinado sugar

dried fruit

heavy cream

Combine oats, salt, and water and bring to a boil. Reduce heat to a gentle boil and cook for 45 minutes or so, or until the oats have thickened up and are soft to the bite. Oats can cook pretty much unattended for the first 20 minutes or so; once they start to thicken, check in on them from time to time to make sure none are sticking to the bottom and burning.

Ladle into shallow bowls and scatter turbinado sugar and dried fruit across the tops. Finish each bowl with a tablespoon of cream.

savory oatmeal

serves 4–6

We've gotten accustomed to oatmeal as a sweet dish but there's no reason not to make a savory version—it's just another grain, like rice or grits, and it takes to savory applications well. This is a simple recipe that uses oats as a background for seasonal vegetables, but you could also use these oats as the foundation for braised rabbit or duck or a hearty stew.

2 cups steel-cut oats

7 cups water

1 tsp kosher salt

1 tsp turbinado sugar

1 tbsp unsalted butter

black pepper

2 cups prepared seasonal vegetables

1/4 cups grated hard cheese optional

Combine oats, water, salt, and sugar in a medium-sized (3-quart) pot. Bring to a boil, then turn down to a gentle boil. Cook for about 30–40 minutes, stirring occasionally until most of the water has been absorbed and the oats are just tender. Add more salt to taste, stir in butter, and crack in a bit of black pepper.

Spoon the oats into four shallow bowls and add vegetables evenly among the bowls. Add grated cheese if desired. You can really send this dish over the top by adding a sunny or poached egg.

RECOMMENDED SEASONAL VEGETABLES

SPRING
Sautéed snap peas
Fresh spinach leaves
Radish slices (braised or raw)
Broccoli rabe

SUMMER
Roasted cherry tomatoes
Corn (roasted or raw)
Blanched green beans
Sautéed mushrooms
Braised small onions

FALL
Roasted cauliflower
Roasted brussels sprouts
Sautéed chard
Roasted pumpkin or squash
Shredded kale

WINTER
Roasted butternut or acorn squash
Roasted celery root
Roasted parsnips or carrots
Shredded kale
Raw spinach or maché
Roasted garlic

savory oatmeal with sunnyside-up egg (page 26)

granola

On those mornings when you don't want to do anything but get up, pour coffee, and sit with your face in the sun, homemade granola is a good thing to have around. Ours is meant to be not too sweet. We serve it over very tangy plain yogurt from upstate New York's Ronnybrook Farm Dairy and add a swirl of local honey for people who want it a little sweeter.

yields 5 cups

2 1/2 cups rolled oats

1/2 cup raw wheat germ

1/2 cup flax seed

1/2 cup sesame seeds

1 cup blanched almonds, chopped

1 scant tsp cinnamon

1/8 tsp kosher salt

1/8 tsp black pepper

1/4 cup + 2 tbsp (3 oz) canola oil

3 tbsp honey

3 tbsp molasses

1/4 cup dried fruit

Heat oven to 300°F.

Combine all dry ingredients in a large bowl and mix well. Add the canola oil, honey, and molasses (if you measure the oil in your measuring cup first, the honey and molasses will pour more easily). Stir until well combined and all the dry ingredients are coated.

Spread the granola on a baking sheet with a spatula—if you like your granola with clusters, make sure it's packed together tightly.

Bake for 10 minutes before stirring. If you want to preserve clusters, just be sure you don't stir it too thoroughly.

Continue baking and stirring every 10 minutes until the granola is golden brown—about 30–35 minutes. Remove the pan from the oven and add dried fruit. Allow the granola to cool completely (it will get crunchy as it cools). Store in an airtight container for up to 2 weeks.

(quick and) dirty rice

serves 6

This is a quick-and-dirty version of dirty rice, great for using up leftover rice and meat from the previous night's dinner. It's a nice change from your usual breakfast grains, and it's delicious and versatile.

Don't feel constrained by this particular combination of ingredients and feel free to use whatever you have on hand.

2 pieces of bacon

1–2 pieces of sausage

1–2 chicken livers, roughly chopped optional

1 leek, trimmed and sliced across the stalk into thin ribbons

1 cup chicken stock or water

3 cups cooked rice

1 1/2 cups cooked chicken, pork, duck, or turkey, shredded

5–6 pieces dried fruit, chopped

1/4 cup flat-leaf parsley leaves, chopped

kosher salt

black pepper

Cook bacon in a pan big enough to eventually hold all the rice and meat. When it's crispy and has rendered its fat, remove the bacon and hold it on a paper towel while you cook the rest of the ingredients.

Pour out all but about a tablespoon of bacon fat from the pan and add the sausage pieces and chicken livers (if using). Cook until they've started to brown, then add the leek to the pan and reduce heat to medium low.

Once the leek has softened, add 1–2 tablespoons chicken stock or water to loosen up any meat that's stuck to the bottom of the pan. Finally add the cooked rice, shredded meat, and dried fruit. Add enough stock or water, about 1/2–3/4 cup, to loosen up the rice but not so much you turn it into soup. (A half a cup should be plenty.)

When the rice and meat are hot and the dried fruit is slightly plumped up by the cooking, remove the pan from heat. Crumble the bacon and add it to the pan with fine parsley. Stir, season to taste with salt and pepper, and serve. Top with a sunnyside-up egg if desired—this dish is delicious with a yolk running into it.

farro salad

serves 6

Because we usually eat wheat only when it's been milled into flour, it's easy to forget that it's a grain like oats or corn. But recently farmers have been bringing back ancient varieties of wheat, like farro. If you can't find farro, conventional wheat berries will do just fine for this dish—both are delicious.

1 cup farro or wheat berries

2 cups water

kosher salt

1 lemon

1/4 cup vegetable oil

black pepper

1–2 crisp apples Gala or Fuji are good options

1 bunch lacinato kale

1/2 cup dried cranberries

1 cup spiced pecans page 158

Wash the farro or wheat berries in a sieve before adding to a 4–6-quart pot with 2 cups of water and a pinch of salt. Bring to a boil, stir, and reduce heat to a simmer. Cook covered until water is absorbed and the farro is swollen and tender, 45–50 minutes. Remove from heat and spread onto a sheet pan to cool.

Cut and squeeze the lemon into a small bowl, removing any seeds. Slowly whisk in the vegetable oil until you've got a viscous and balanced dressing. Season with salt and pepper.

Wash and dice the apple.

Wash and trim the kale, cutting out the thick parts of the spine. Stack the leaves on top of one another and cut into thin ribbons (you'll be eating them raw, so you want to cut them into pieces you'd be happy eating).

In a large bowl, combine the cooled farro, the kale, the diced apple, and the cranberries. Stir well to combine and add dressing so that it's well distributed through the salad. Finally, add the pecans and stir to mix in well. Taste for seasoning, adjust if necessary, and serve.

pastries

Pastries are, as a rule, overrepresented at the breakfast table, and in every breakfast cookbook, tempting you to imagine yourself in a world in which you get up at 3:00 a.m. like a classical pastry chef to pile your table high with fresh sticky buns and berry galettes.

I like a croissant as much as anyone, but I've always felt like the emphasis on fancy pastries for breakfast keeps people from taking more practical measures to feed themselves well in the mornings. The emphasis here is on quick breads (like biscuits and pancakes) and pastries that keep well, so that you can make them one day and eat them all week.

biscuits

yield 14–18 biscuits

Here's a dirty little secret: Biscuits are almost the easiest thing you'll ever bake. But that's a significant "almost," because while the recipe for biscuits is as simple as tying your shoe, executing it is another story. Your goal is to hit the perfect midpoint between extreme delicacy on the one hand and structure and strength on the other. You need to work quickly, with a light hand, to keep your biscuits light and delicate, but not so delicate that your biscuits crumble in your hands when you pick them up. You need to work the dough enough that your biscuits have some structure and hold together when you slather them with butter and jam—but not to work them so long that they become dense and chewy. If your dough starts to feel elastic or springy, you've gone too far.

It takes practice to get biscuits right. The good news is that your trials will still taste good, especially when they're fresh from the oven. The recipe is simple enough that you can try it once a week without putting yourself out much.

Keep all ingredients cold and dry while you work

3 1/4 cups (1 lb) pastry flour

2 cups (10 oz) bleached all-purpose flour

3 tbsp baking powder

1 tbsp kosher salt

1 tbsp turbinado sugar

6 oz cold butter, cut into small pieces

2 1/2 cups soured milk
to sour, add 2 1/2 tbsp apple cider vinegar to 2 3/8 cups milk

Preheat oven to 500°F.

In a large bowl, combine the flours, baking powder, salt, and sugar and blend well.

Toss the butter pieces into the flour and blend well with your fingers—you'll squeeze and pinch the butter into the flour until it's well mixed and no piece of butter is larger than the fingernail on your smallest finger. The flour should resemble cornmeal. You want to do this step as quickly as possible so the butter does not begin to melt, but be thorough: Getting the butter right is your best hedge against tough biscuits.

Add 2 1/4 cups of the soured milk to the flour and butter. Working quickly, mix the milk in with a rubber spatula, mixing only until the dough begins to hold together. If the mix seems dry, add the last 1/4 cup of milk.

Dump the dough onto a floured work surface. Gather it together and pat briefly to flatten. Fold the dough over on itself three or four times, then pat into a rough rectangle about 1 1/2-inch thick. Use a bench scraper to ensure the dough isn't sticking to the table.

>>

Dip a 2 1/2-inch biscuit cutter in a little flour before pressing it into the dough. Lift the cut biscuit out without twisting the cutter and place on a well-buttered baking sheet. Biscuits should be almost touching. Brush tops lightly with soured milk. Repeat until you've used all of the dough.

Bake for 15–20 minutes, until the biscuits are golden, well risen and light. If they feel wet or heavy, bake them longer.

pancakes

serves 4–6 hungry people

There's nothing more tempting than a stack of pancakes crowned by slowly melting butter and maple syrup. And there's nothing more disappointing than the pancakes you get at most restaurants: dense, cakey discs made worse by the acrid bite of excess baking powder. I've eaten hundreds of them, at summer camp and at church pancake dinners. They were—all of them, all the time—awful.

I was raised on more delicate pancakes, which we called "pig's feet pancakes" because they were made from the same batter my grandfather fried his trotters in. They weren't always perfect circles, and—because my mother was forever fending off the demands of four noisy children—they were often burned around the edges. But they were light, crunchy at the edges, and like clouds in the middle. Those were the pancakes I was wanted to re-create at Egg.

We rely on eggs to do most of the leavening work here, and let the baking powder play a supporting role. We mix the batter lightly so that we don't develop too much gluten, which makes pancakes tough. And we keep the batter a little thinner than you might expect, which means our pancakes don't always cook up perfectly round or puffy—but they are more than delicious enough to make up for it.

4 large eggs

2 1/2 cups milk

2 tbsp vanilla

6 tbsp (3 oz) unsalted butter, melted plus 2 tbsp for cooking

2 1/4 cups flour

1 tsp kosher salt

1 heaping tbsp baking powder

1/4 cup turbinado sugar

In a medium bowl, combine eggs, milk, and vanilla and whip until foamy. Add the melted butter to the eggs, milk, and vanilla, and mix well.

In a large bowl, combine the flour, salt, baking powder, and sugar, and blend well (a whisk is useful here). Add the egg mixture to the flour mixture and blend lightly with a whisk. Batter will still be slightly lumpy.

Heat a griddle over medium heat (to 350°F if you have a thermometer) or until it is hot enough to melt butter without browning it. Put a teaspoon of butter in the griddle before adding the pancakes. For each pancake, scoop 1/4 cup of batter onto the skillet, and cook the pancakes about 3 minutes on the first side, or until bubbles begin rising through the surface of the pancake. Then flip and cook 2 minutes on the other side.

It's important not to flip the pancakes again—flipping them again just flattens them out. You can tell the pancakes are finished by putting your hand gently on top of one and pushing it very slightly to the side. If the top of the pancake slides over without moving the bottom of the pancake, keep cooking.

french toast

French toast is probably the most decadent thing we have on the menu at Egg. We start with loaves of brioche from Amy's, a now-legendary bakery in Manhattan. Then we make a custard that tastes like melted vanilla ice cream, cook the two together until they're golden brown, and hit them with excellent butter and maple syrup.

serves 5–6

6 eggs

2 cups whole milk

2 cups heavy cream

2 1/2 tbsp vanilla

2 1/2 tbsp maple syrup

1 pinch kosher salt

nutmeg or cinnamon

4 tbsp unsalted butter

5–6 pieces of challah or brioche, sliced 1-inch thick

Preheat oven to 200°F.

Crack eggs into a large bowl and whisk until thoroughly blended (if ou don't mix the eggs well, you'll get strands of egg in your toast). Add all of the rest of the ingredients except bread and butter, including a grating or two of fresh nutmeg (you could also use cinnamon; I just happen to hate cinnamon) and blend well.

Heat a skillet over medium-low heat. Add one teaspoon of butter and swirl the pan to coat it as the butter melts. You want the butter to melt and foam but not to brown.

Dip a slice of bread into the custard mix. If your bread is fresh and airy, dip it quickly—it'll soak up fast. If it's stale or dense, let it hang out in there for a few seconds to soak up the custard. As you remove it, allow any excess to drip back into the bowl. Place the slice of bread in the middle of the skillet.

Allow the bread to cook undisturbed for a minute, then check the bottom to make sure it's not burning. Once the bottom of the bread is golden brown (2 or 3 minutes) turn it onto the other side. Let the toast cook undisturbed for 2 minutes. To check for doneness, press lightly on the top of the bread with the back of a spatula. If custard seeps out, let the toast keep cooking. Repeat these steps with all the slices.

Place each slice in the preheated oven to keep them warm as you prepare the rest. When you're ready to eat, remove the slices from the oven and serve them with additional butter and maple syrup.

cornbread

serves 10–12 as a side dish

At a wedding in North Carolina, a friend emerged from the buffet tent into the field where most of us stood listening to an impromptu bluegrass band by a bonfire. She had a plate of macaroni and cheese and pulled pork, but she looked disappointed. "They got Yankee cornbread in there," she said.

"Yankee cornbread" meant sweet and bready—whereas proper cornbread is savory and crumbly. This classic recipe makes a crumbly, delicious bread that's good with molasses poured over it or under a bowl of stew. You need a 12-inch cast-iron skillet to make this recipe, but you should own one anyway.

4 cups coarse cornmeal

1 tsp baking powder

1 tsp baking soda

1 tbsp kosher salt

3 cups soured milk page 72

2 large eggs, beaten

1 1/2 cups unsalted butter, melted, divided

Preheat oven to 400°F. Put your cast-iron skillet in the oven until very hot.

In a bowl, combine the cornmeal, baking powder, baking soda, and salt and mix until combined.

In a separate bowl, mix the soured milk, beaten eggs, and half the melted butter. Then pour the milk mixture into the cornmeal mixture and mix lightly just until the dry ingredients are moistened. (The batter will be very loose.)

Carefully pull the cast-iron pan out of the oven (or better yet: slide the rack it's on out far enough that you can reach the pan without taking it out). Pour the rest of the melted butter into the skillet, allow it to foam up, and then dump the batter into the pan. Butter will rise up all around the batter, but that's okay—the bread will almost fry in the pan. Give the pan a careful shake to settle the batter, and bake for 30 minutes. The middle of the cornbread will be set and the edges will be golden brown.

Carefully turn the bread out of the pan onto a rack or plate and allow to cool. Cut into wedges to serve.

johnnycakes

serves 4

For a somewhat more rustic alternative to pancakes, try johnnycakes. They're excellent when served as you would pancakes—with butter and maple syrup—but they're also great as the base or a side for a savory meal: you could serve them with scallops and vegetables or with a salad. They're also gluten-free, making them an excellent option for folks who don't eat wheat.

4 tbsp cold, unsalted butter, cut into pieces
plus 1 tbsp unsalted butter for cooking

1 tbsp turbinado sugar

2 cups stone-ground cornmeal

1 tsp kosher salt

1 cup whole milk

1/4 cup boiling water

In a medium bowl, combine the cold butter and sugar. Using a hand-mixer, beat on medium speed until they are well combined and the butter is light and airy, 2–3 minutes. Add the cornmeal and salt and beat 1 minute. Add the milk, then add the boiling water to make a moist but cohesive batter. The batter will thicken as it sits, so if you make it to use later, just thin with water as needed before cooking.

Drop large spoonfuls or an 1/8 cup measure onto a hot, buttered griddle, and flatten slightly with the back of a spoon. Brown evenly, then turn and cook through on the other side, 2–2 1/2 minutes per side.

pound cake

serves 8–12

This was my mother's standard dessert—whenever we needed a cake and she didn't have time to make something fancy, she'd bang out a pound cake to serve with ice cream and custard. It was perfectly good as a dessert, but I liked it best the next morning when she would toast it with salted butter for our breakfast.

Pound cake keeps well, so you can have it for breakfast day after day—if you can make it last that long.

2 sticks (1/2 lb) unsalted butter, cold, cut into pieces

1 2/3 cups white sugar

1/2 tsp kosher salt

5 eggs

2 cups flour, sifted, divided measure after sifting

1 tbsp vanilla

Preheat oven to 350°F. Lightly butter and flour a 10-inch ring pan. Set aside.

In the bowl of a stand mixer, cream the butter and sugar on medium speed until light and airy, 8–10 minutes. Add salt and continue mixing.

While mixing, add 3 of the eggs, one at a time, and mix until they're well incorporated.

Add 2 tablespoons of the flour and blend well. Then add the remaining 2 eggs, one at a time as before. Mix in the rest of the flour, adding it in batches, 1/2 cup at a time. Add vanilla, mixing until just combined. Batter should be silky and light.

Spoon the batter into a prepared ring pan. Bake in center of oven for 45 minutes or until cake is golden brown, springs back when gently touched, and a toothpick inserted in center of cake comes out clean.

Take the cake out of the oven and leave in the pan for 10 minutes. Then carefully remove it from the pan and allow to cool completely on a rack.

blueberry grunt

During my childhood summers, we'd often be in the fortunate position of having more blueberries than we knew what to do with. That's when my mother would make this cake for us to eat morning, noon, and night.

generously serves 9

2 2/3 cups cake flour, divided

2 tsp baking powder

1/2 tsp kosher salt

2 sticks (1/2 lb) unsalted butter

2 cups turbinado sugar

4 eggs

1 cup milk

1 1/2 tsp vanilla

1 quart blueberries

Preheat oven to 350°F. Lightly butter and flour a 9x13-inch pan.

In a large bowl, sift together 2 1/3 cups of the cake flour, baking powder, and salt. Set aside.

Beat butter and sugar together with an electric mixer at medium speed until they are light and creamed. Reduce the speed to low, then add the eggs, one at a time, being sure that each egg is fully incorporated before adding the next. Add the dry ingredients in thirds, alternating with 1/3 cup of the milk. Add vanilla. Finally, toss the blueberries with the reserved 1/3 cup of flour and fold them into the cake mixture.

Bake for 50 minutes, rotating after 25 minutes, until a tester comes out clean and the cake springs back slightly when gently touched. Most of the blueberries will sink to the bottom of the pan as the cake cooks.

lemon cornmeal cake

serves 6–8

If you like your cornbread sweet, fine. But then call it what it is—a cake. This makes an excellent light breakfast with coffee or juice.

3/4 cup finely ground cornmeal

3 tbsp all-purpose flour

3/4 tsp baking powder

1/2 tsp kosher salt

2 large eggs

1/2 cup white sugar

zest of 1 lemon

1/3 cup + 1 tbsp olive oil

2 tbsp milk

1 1/2 tsp fresh lemon juice

3 1/2 tbsp melted unsalted butter

1 tbsp turbinado sugar

Preheat oven to 350°F.

Sift together cornmeal, flour, baking powder, and salt.

In the bowl of a stand mixer, whisk together eggs, sugar, and zest. Set over a small pot of hot water, double-boiler style, and whisk until warm to touch, about 2 minutes. Transfer the bowl to the mixer fitted with whisk attachment and beat on medium speed until it thickens and lightens in color, and forms ribbons when the whisk is lifted, about 5–6 minutes.

In another bowl, combine oil, milk, and lemon juice. Return mixer to medium speed and drizzle this into egg mixture. Reduce to low speed and add the combined cornmeal, flour, baking powder, and salt. Finally, drizzle in melted butter and combine.

Line an 8-inch metal loaf pan with parchment paper. Pour batter into pan and bake for 40–45 minutes, rotating once. Test for doneness by inserting a toothpick or the tip of a sharp knife into the center of the cake—it should come out clean, and the cake should spring back when gently touched.

Remove cake from the oven and immediately sprinkle the sugar on top. Place pan on a rack to cool for 10 minutes. Carefully lift cake out of the pan and return it to the rack to finish cooling.

pecan pie

It's a low-water mark for breakfast when you find yourself guiltily grabbing a packaged miniature pecan pie and burned, oversized coffee from the checkout at the gas station where you've filled up your car. But let's be real: We've all done it, or thought of it.

In its essence, it's not such a bad idea. It's just that prepackaged food is depressing, gas station coffee is depressing, and eating your breakfast while you sit in traffic crawling to work is depressing. Redeem it all with a pie made right and enjoy it at home. This pie keeps well, so you can make it on Sunday and eat it before work all week long.

makes one 9-inch pie

1/2 recipe pie crust page 93

3 eggs, well-beaten in a large bowl, divided

1 cup + 1 tbsp white sugar

2 tbsp (2 oz) unsalted butter, melted

2/3 cup light corn syrup

1/4 cup maple syrup

1 tsp vanilla

pinch kosher salt

2 cups chopped pecans + 1/4 lb whole pecans for top

Preheat oven to 350°F and place rack in lower third of the oven.

Roll out the pie crust on a lightly floured board to 13 inches to fit into a 9-inch pie pan. Crimp the edge and refrigerate while preparing filling.

Remove 2 teaspoons of beaten eggs and combine with 1 teaspoon water to make an egg wash. Divide the sugar into two equal parts: mix one half with the eggs and the other half with the melted butter.

When the sugar is well mixed with the eggs and the butter, combine both sugar mixtures. Add the corn syrup, maple syrup, vanilla, and salt. Stir to combine. Stir in the chopped pecans. Remove the pie crust from the fridge and pour the filling into the crust. Brush the exposed edge of the crust with egg wash and garnish the top of the pie with whole pecans in a pattern that pleases you (we cover the entire top with nuts in concentric circles)

Bake for 60–65 minutes, or until a knife inserted into the center of the pie comes out clean. Keep a watch on the pie after about 40 minutes. If the edges of the crust appear to be getting too brown, cover them lightly with foil. Allow to cool completely before eating. Store loosely covered in the fridge.

strawberry-rhubarb pie

yields one 9-inch pie

Another pie for breakfast? It sounds decadent, but this one's not really that different from a biscuit slathered with jelly—so why not?

1 recipe pie crust page 92

1 1/2 lbs rhubarb, trimmed and cut into 1/2-inch slices

1 lb strawberries, hulled and cut into pieces
the size of the rhubarb

1/2 cup white sugar

1/2 cup light brown sugar

1 tbsp lemon juice

zest of 1 lemon

5 tbsp (1/3 cup) cornstarch

1/2 tsp kosher salt

pinch of black pepper

1 tbsp (1/2 oz) cold unsalted butter, cut into small cubes

1 egg mixed with 1 tbsp water for egg wash

Preheat oven to 425°F with a rimmed baking sheet on a rack in lower third of the oven.

On a lightly floured board, roll out a piece of dough large enough for the bottom crust (13 inches). Pat it into a pie tin and place in the refrigerator. Roll out another piece of similar size (11 inches) and with a pastry cutter or sharp knife, cut it into 1/2-inch strips. Cover with plastic wrap and set aside.

In a large bowl, mix the rhubarb, strawberries, sugars, lemon juice and zest, cornstarch, salt, and pepper and toss to combine. A little syrup will form in the bottom of the bowl. Taste to see how tart it is: Depending on the time of year and the sweetness of your fuit, it may need more sugar.

Remove pie crust from refrigerator. Pile all the rhubarb-strawberry mixture into your pie crust—it should be very full. Dot the top with butter and lay the other strips of crust across the top in a lattice pattern. Brush the top of the pie with the egg wash and place pie in the oven on the preheated baking sheet. (The fruit gives off a lot of juice and the pan will catch the drips). Bake for 15 minutes. Then reduce oven temperature to 375°F and continue baking for an additional 60 minutes. The crust will be nicely golden. Remove the pie from the oven and place on a rack to cool for 1 hour before slicing.

pie crust

A simple but useful pie crust recipe
to use with our strawberry-rhubarb or
pecan pies.

makes one double-crust 9-inch pie

2 1/2 cups all-purpose flour

8 tbsp (1 stick) unsalted butter, cold, cut into 1/2-inch cubes

3/4 tsp of kosher salt

Yolk of 1 egg, beaten

1 tsp apple cider vinegar

3/4 cup ice water

In a food processor, combine the flour, butter, and salt and pulse two or three times until the mixture resembles a coarse meal. There should be pebbles of butter throughout the mixture.

Add the egg yolk and vinegar to 3/4 cup ice water and stir to combine. Drizzle 4 tablespoons of this mixture over the dough and gently stir or pulse to combine. Gather a golf ball-size bit of dough and squeeze to combine. If it does not hold together, add a little more of the liquid (3 tablespoons should do it) and stir or pulse two to three times, then check again.

Turn the dough out onto a lightly floured surface and gather together into a rough ball. You want to be careful not to overwork the flour, but not too careful—the dough should hold together. Divide the ball in half with a knife or a pastry scraper, then divide each portion in half again, and again, to create eight portions. Using the heel of your hand, flatten each portion of dough once or twice to expand the pebbles of butter, then gather the dough together again in one ball. Divide this ball in half.

Flatten each ball into a 5- or 6-inch disc and dust lightly with flour. Wrap the discs in plastic wrap and place in the refrigerator for at least 60 minutes.

When ready to use, remove from refrigerator and allow to sit at room temperature for 5–10 minutes before rolling.

coffee cake

generously serves 9

I can live without cinnamon rolls and sticky buns and muffins, but not without coffee cake. I grew up eating it every Christmas morning, and every other morning we were lucky enough to get it.

TOPPING (YIELDS 3 1/2 CUPS)

6 oz unsalted butter, softened

3/4 cup flour

1 1/2 cups light brown sugar, lightly packed

1 1/2 tbsp cinnamon

1 1/2 cups pecans, chopped

CAKE

3 cups flour

4 tsp baking powder

1 tsp kosher salt

3 egg whites

6 oz unsalted butter, softened

1 1/2 cups turbinado sugar

1 1/2 cups hot whole milk steeped with 2 tbsp ground coffee strained and cooled yielding 1 1/4 cups coffee-infused milk

Preheat oven to 350°F.

In a large bowl, combine topping ingredients. Rub butter into dry ingredients until the mixture is well combined and crumbly.

Sift together flour, baking powder, and salt. In a separate bowl, beat egg whites until stiff, but not dry.

In a mixer, beat butter and sugar together until the combination is light and well blended, about 3 minutes. Slowly add flour mixture and milk alternately in small batches until combined. Use a spatula to fold in beaten egg whites. Gently spread the batter into a shallow greased and floured 9x13-inch baking pan. Sprinkle half of the topping over the batter.

After 30 minutes of baking add another sprinkling of topping.

Bake for a total of 40–45 minutes, or until the cake is no longer jiggly and a toothpick inserted into the center of the cake comes out clean.

Allow the cake to cool for 30–45 minutes if you can stand it—it'll be very delicate when it's hot.

spoonbread

Spoonbread is a special occasion dish, a kind of rustic soufflé that's great as a side to savory dishes that generate a good sauce: the spoon bread laps up the sauce and becomes a kind of cloud of flavor. It's also great just with honey at breakfast. This is my grandmother's recipe.

serves 4–6 as a side

1 tsp unsalted butter

2 tbsp all-purpose flour

3 eggs, separated

2 cups whole milk

1/2 cups fine-ground cornmeal

1/2 tsp baking powder

1/2 tsp kosher salt

Preheat oven to 350°F. Lightly butter a 9-inch soufflé dish and dust with flour.

Whisk or beat the egg whites until peaks just hold their shape. Set aside.

Beat the egg yolks until light.

Heat the milk nearly to boiling, then stir in cornmeal gradually. Cook until the mixture has the consistency of mush, about 5–7 minutes, then remove from heat and add baking powder, salt, and the egg yolks. Fold in the egg whites and pour into the soufflé dish. Bake for 30 minutes, until the mixture is risen and stable, and serve at once. Don't get bent out of shape if it falls. It'll still be delicious.

winter breakfast (page 114)

meat, poultry, and seafood

There are only a few forms of meat that have a familiar place at the breakfast table. We eat bacon, sausage, ham, and the occasional piece of steak, but rarely consider other meat for morning consumption.

It's not so strange, really: breakfast meats need to be quick to prepare so that you're not spending your entire morning getting them ready. But a lot of meat dishes—braises and stews in particular—can be prepared the night before (or several nights before). Reheat them in the morning, and you've got a full breakfast in one pot in 10 minutes.

A lot of the recipes in this chapter are pretty involved compared to the rest of the book. They're something to do on a weekend afternoon, for example, that make your weekday breakfasts simple yet fulfilling. We include recipes for chicken, beef, and pork dishes that you can make in one day and then eat all week. We've got bacon and sausage recipes, as well as recipes for fried oysters and smoked fish.

But for us, country ham—America's great cured meat—rises above them all. If you had only one meat in your breakfast pantry, country ham would be the one to keep. It's versatile and delicious and fascinating.

on country ham

At my grandmother's farm there were many small outbuildings whose original purpose had been eclipsed by the need to store lawnmowers, footballs, spare tires, grills. The old bathhouse was a toolshed by the time I got to know it; the kitchen stored busted furniture that was too precious to throw out. The building that once housed my great-great-uncle's law practice now houses fishing tackle and a Ping-Pong table. And next to the Ping-Pong house was the one building that we almost never opened, whose purpose I never heard discussed. It was the smokehouse, where all the hams and bacon that had fed the farm for its first 100 years had been hung. I got a peek inside it one day when I was in elementary school: a cast-iron cauldron on a dirt floor, smoke-blackened beams still festooned with wires that once held cuts of pig, a few old jaw bones still dangling overhead. The room still smelled of smoke, though it had probably been 20 years since the last fire had been kindled inside.

After that glimpse, I didn't go back in that building for 30 years. In the meantime, I learned to love country ham as any Southern church boy is bound to. It was served at every covered-dish dinner, usually tucked into a buttered Parker House roll or a biscuit. This was a simple but serious pleasure, a buttery roll cut by a sharp bite of salty ham. At church picnics, I'd load up on them because while I never knew whether I could trust someone else's fried chicken not to be dry, or someone else's mac and cheese not to be bland, I was pretty sure that no one could screw up country ham and a roll. Of the many things that were exciting about opening Egg, bringing country ham to Brooklyn was near the top of the list. We were still in the grips of prosciutto mania back in 2005, but people were beginning to wake up to the fact that there were other cured hams in the world worth trying.

When I was testing recipes before I opened Egg, I bought and cooked a Smithfield, the staple of every Southern table I've ever eaten at. It had been cured for maybe three months and it was as salty and dry and pink as I remembered from childhood. I tried it out on a couple of friends, who were taken aback by the saltiness. "You'll get used to it," I promised, "and you won't want to stop."

>>

But then, on a lark, I ordered a ham from Nancy Newsom, a ham-maker in western Kentucky who uses her grandfather's recipe and smokehouse to make traditional long-aged hams. The first bite of her ham gave me a whole new sense of what country ham could be. They were cured for over a year, subjected to all the vagaries of Kentucky's weather and the magic of an old ham house. It was salty, sure, but that was just the beginning of it: it was funky and moody; the fat on it was translucent and fragrant. I wanted to eat every part of it.

I felt a twinge of a traitor's guilt when I called to place my first order for hams from Kentucky—after all, I grew up calling them Virginia hams. But Nancy's voice put me at ease—it sounded just like home, even though she was in a different time zone. And her hams took me back to a time and place I'd never actually been able to live. They made me think differently of that building at the farm. Maybe we didn't use it not because we had no use for it, but because it was the one place too sacred to defile with lawn chairs and flat tires.

buying and using country ham

It's worth the trouble to seek out a proper country ham, one that's been cured in salt and aged for at least a year by someone who cares. Newsom's are excellent. Benton's and Edwards are also incredible.

When you unwrap one, take a minute to appreciate what you have in front of you. It should be dark and dense. It may well show some signs of mold—that's a good sign. Just brush it off with a damp rag or a brush and get to cooking.

There are a couple of ways you can happily cook a country ham, and we've outlined both of them in the recipe that follows. But there are a few things to bear in mind no matter which method you choose to cook yours:

1.   Use every last bit of your ham. It's all delicious, and the parts you can't eat (see page 108) can go into making something else delicious. Make a stock out of the bone and any leftover meats—add just a few aromatic vegetables and you'll have a broth so delicious you'll want to use it in everything from soup to pasta sauce.

2.   Don't be shy about the fat. It's too delicious to waste.

3.   Think of your ham as a seasoning, like a spice or a relish—shave a little onto your dinner plate at any meal to enliven your beans or your grits or your fish. My mother recalls growing up with a country ham on the sideboard all the time, there for the picking.

preparing country ham

Country ham is already cured, and you could eat it as it comes, as you do prosciutto. But traditionally, American country hams are cooked before they're put to use.

We deal with country ham in the simplest possible way. You'll see all kinds of recipes for cooking country hams with spices or molasses or even Coca-Cola; you'll be exhorted to soak your ham overnight to leach out salt; you'll be instructed to glaze your hams with something sweet. You can do any of those things if you like, but you'll do just fine without them if your ham is good.

Choose one of the following methods based on what you can manage on your stove and want out of your ham. If you roast it, you'll end up with a crackling skin and a ham fit for the center of your dinner table. The boiling method is simpler, but requires a huge pot; if you boil it, the skin will be pliable and pale, but you'll have an incredible stock to use for stews or sauces.

>>

roasting method

Rinse your ham in cold water and scrub off any mold or funk. Preheat the oven to 300ºF. Remove one rack and put the other on the oven's lowest level.

Put the ham on a rack in a roasting pan. Pour a cup of hot tap water into the bottom of the pan, then cover the pan with aluminum foil.

Put the ham in the oven and let it roast for 3–4 hours. Check on the ham by peeling back the foil at the hock end and jiggling the hock. If it's even a little loose, your ham is done. If it's not, return the pan to the oven for 20 minutes (make sure there's still some liquid in the bottom of the pan. If there's not, add another cup of hot water or the drippings will burn).

The ham is done when the bone at the hock end is slightly loose. Remove the pan to the stove top or a heatproof surface. Remove all the aluminum foil so that the skin doesn't steam and get soft and you can inhale the incredible aromas rising from the ham. Allow to cool then follow the instructions below on skinning and slicing the ham.

(Your roasting pan should have a layer of rich drippings in it—they are worth saving. Skim away any fat and foam and discard; save the jelly-like drippings from the pan in a container in the fridge. Add a teaspoon or two to soups to give them a magical boost.)

Peel back the skin by using your fingers or the point of a paring knife to slice around the edge of the skin—you want to go in parallel with the surface of the skin so that you're leaving as much fat as possible on the body of the ham. (Even if you don't want to eat the fat, you should strive to leave it on the ham to keep the ham from drying out.) The skin should peel back pretty easily in one solid piece, like the carapace of a beetle. To slice the ham, make a first cut perpendicular to the surface of the ham a couple of inches up from the bottom of the hock, right where the ham starts to widen. Make a second cut just a fraction of an inch farther up the ham from that, but slightly angled down so that it meets your first cut near the bone (it's a little like cutting a wedge in a tree you're trying to fell). You may have to wiggle the knife a bit to get this first slice to slip out, but it gets easier from here, and now you've got a snack to tide you over while you work at it.

For each subsequent slice, follow the line of the most recent cut, making your next cut just a sliver north of it. Country ham is best in thin slices, so try to keep your knife steady and your cuts smooth and even. As you cut more and more ham, you'll find your slices getting larger. Stop when you have enough, fold the skin back over the ham, and let it be until you need another bite. That moment will come sooner than you think.

boiling method

Rinse your ham in cold water and scrub off any mold or funk.

Put the ham in a pot large enough to hold the ham and the water you need to cover it. Add enough water to cover the ham (if the hock—the narrow end—sticks out by an inch or two that's okay). Put on a burner you won't need for the next couple of hours. Bring to a boil over high heat, then turn down to a very low boil (just above a simmer) and cook until the hock bone is slightly loose when you wiggle it.

Carefully remove the ham from the pot—be careful! You might want to get help with this. Put the ham somewhere to cool where it won't be molested by your dog. Skim any foam or particles off the top of the water you cooked the ham in and bring back to a simmer. You can let this cook until it's reduced by a half. Store the reduced stock in the refrigerator, or divide and freeze. Slice ham as described above.

country ham biscuits

serves 4

4 biscuits page 72

2 tbsp butter

8 oz country ham, thinly sliced (about 3 cups) page 100

6 oz sharp cheddar cheese, grated

2 tbsp + 2 tsp fig jam, divided page 184

If I had to eat only one thing from our menu for the rest of my life, this would be it: salty, sweet, pungent, and rich. The combination of salty country ham and buttery biscuit digs into a deep seam of childhood memory. The dried fig jam adds a nod to the figs that grow all over the beaches of North Carolina, while the aged cheddar acknowledges one of the great foods of the Northeast, where we live now. I like how everything inside this biscuit is aged: the ham, the figs, the cheese.

Preheat oven to 450°F.

Split the biscuits and place on a baking sheet. Put a piece of butter on each side.

Next to the biscuits on the same baking sheet, divide the ham into four piles and cover with cheddar. Put the biscuits and ham into the oven and cook until the cheese and butter have melted, about 3 minutes.

To assemble, put a pile of cheese and ham on the bottom half of each biscuit. Add 2 teaspoons of fig jam to the top half, close, and serve.

country ham stock

yields 2 quarts

Even when you've eaten every last bit of salvageable meat from your ham, there's still a world of joy awaiting you in what's left; country ham stock, which is as easy to make as it is delicious.

The simplest way to use your leftover bone and meat scraps is just to throw them in a pot of collards, or a big stew. But you can also cook the bone and scraps in water (with some aromatic vegetables, if you like) and save the resulting broth to give a boost to everything else you eat. You can spike a pasta sauce with it, swirl it into a dish of beans, add a tablespoon to a pan of sautéed greens—you almost can't lose with it.

1 country ham bone + scraps you can include the skin, too, though I'd recommend scraping most of the fat off it first

1 large onion, peeled optional

1 carrot, washed optional

1 celery rib optional

6 cloves garlic, peeled optional

Find a pot big enough to contain the ham bone and scraps. Fill with water to cover the bone by one inch. Add the vegetables, if you're using them.

Bring the water to a simmer and allow to cook for 3–4 hours, skimming occasionally when froth or scum floats to the top.

Remove the bone and vegetables and pour the broth through a cheesecloth or fine sieve. Keep a quart or so in the fridge and freeze the rest in batches to have available whenever needed.

basic bacon

serves 2

6 strips bacon, preferably thick-cut D'Artagnan and Niman Ranch both make good varieties that are widely available

Bacon is so prevalent that it's practically our national meat. But like eggs, bacon can be profoundly disappointing when it's done wrong. It's easy to burn. It's easy to cook it unevenly, so that half of each strip is verging on incinerated while the other half is undercooked, chewy as a pig's ear. But as millions of bacon worshippers will attest, it's worth getting it right. You want a perfect balance between well-crisped edges, streaks of lean, and rich, smoky fat.

Heat a pan just big enough to hold all your bacon over low to medium heat. Add the bacon, laying it out flat, and let it cook slowly until it starts to give up some of its fat, about 3–4 minutes. Then raise the heat to medium and get your bacon sizzling. Turn it from time to time to keep it browning evenly on both sides, and rotate the strips from the middle of the pan to the edges to keep it from settling on any hot spots.

Once the bacon is as crispy as you like it, remove and place on a paper towel briefly to soak up some of the excess fat, then move it to a plate. Don't leave it sitting in its fat on a paper towel or it'll get soft and greasy.

PRO TIP

If you have to cook a lot of bacon, as we do at Egg, cook it on a rimmed baking sheet in a 350°F oven for 15–18 minutes. You can line the strips up close together when they're raw; they'll shrink considerably while they cook. But keep an eye and a timer on that bacon: bacon in the oven will go from undercooked to burned in a heartbeat.

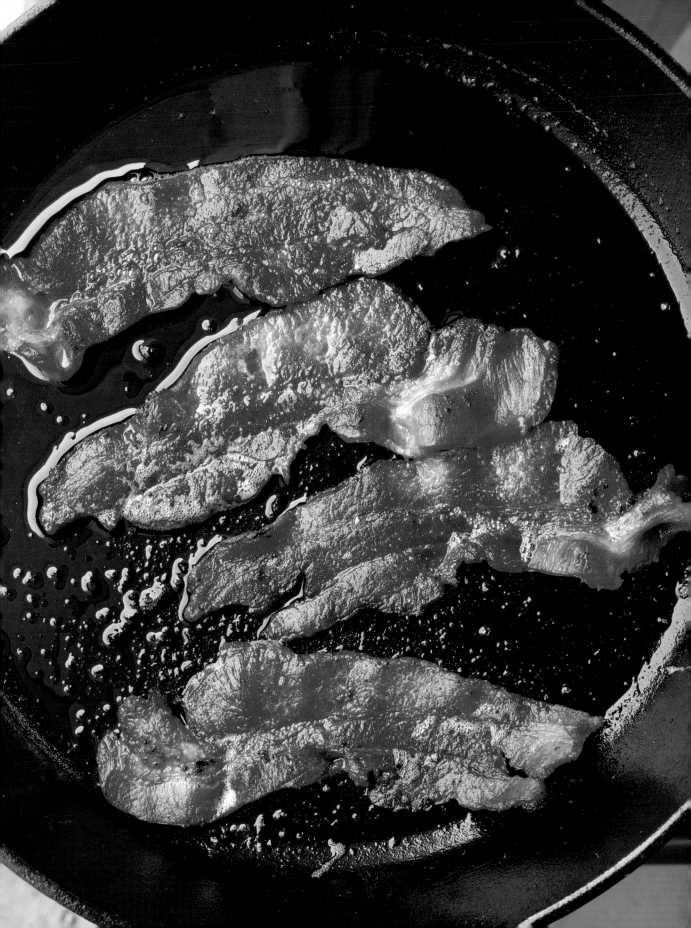

advanced bacon

yields 8 lbs of bacon

---

110 g kosher salt

80 g turbinado sugar

20 g Instacure #1 available online

6 g black peppercorns, coarse ground

4 g coriander seeds, toasted, finely ground

4 g mace, ground

3 g star anise, coarse ground

2 g red pepper flakes

1 9lb pork belly about one belly

If you really love bacon, take a crack at curing and smoking your own. You'll need a cold-smoking setup to do the smoking. If the Internet doesn't yield a good plan for making one, I recommend *Charcuterie* by Brian Polcyn and Michael Ruhlman for all the basics of smoking meat. (If you don't want to mess with smoking, you can still make a delicious unsmoked version of bacon by curing a pork belly as described below.)

Use a digital gram scale to measure ingredients when you're curing meat—it's the best and safest way to get everything right.

This recipe yields enough bacon to last you months. You can divide the cured bacon into 1-lb. pieces and freeze them until you are ready to use.

Mix all ingredients except the pork belly and rub thoroughly on the surface of the meat to coat. Let sit 10 minutes to allow cure to adhere. Lay out sheets of plastic wrap large enough for the belly to sit on, sprinkle half the remaining cure on the plastic wrap. Set the belly on the wrap, cover with remaining cure. Wrap in the plastic very tightly.

Refrigerate for one week, turning once a day. When the meat feels firm to the touch, remove the wrap and brush off the cure. Smoke it slowly with your favorite flavor of woodsmoke for at least 3–4 hours, until internal temperature of 155ºF is reached. Let cool, then cut into slices and cook or freeze for later.

candied bacon

serves 4

Candied bacon is a divisive dish at Egg: to some people, it's an abomination; a gilding of a lily so precious that to alter it in any way is a desecration. To others, it's crack, as addictive as roller coasters and ice cream.

1/4 cup water

1/4 cup turbinado sugar

8 strips bacon, cooked

Combine the water and sugar in a sauté pan just big enough to contain the strips of bacon. Bring to a boil and cook until the sugar dissolves into a syrup. Reduce the heat to low and submerge bacon in the syrup and stir to coat. Remove to a rack to set and eat immediately (or within the hour).

winter breakfast

serves 12

This is a make-ahead breakfast dish. Braise the meat and vegetables the night before you mean to eat them, then enjoy a morning of nearly effortless cooking. This recipe makes quite a bit so you can freeze half the batch if you like.

3 lb pork shoulder, cut into 2-inch cubes

kosher salt

black pepper

crushed red pepper

1-lb slab bacon, cut into 1-inch cubes

1/2 small celery root, diced

1 large parsnip, diced

1 medium carrot, diced

1/2 large yellow onion, diced

2 cloves garlic, roughly chopped

2 quarts country ham stock page 108

Season the shoulder meat generously with salt and black pepper and red pepper flakes and let rest to absorb flavors (up to several hours).

Preheat the oven to 300°F.

In a heavy ovenproof pot (like an enameled stew pot), brown the bacon cubes over medium-high heat, then remove and set aside. Pat the shoulder meat dry with a paper towel and brown it on all sides in the rendered bacon fat. Remove and set aside.

Add all the diced and chopped vegetables to the pot. Use the juices they release to scrape up any residue on the bottom of the pot from cooking the meat (if the residue looks as though it will burn before the vegetables render any juice, use a little water to deglaze the bottom of the pot).

Cook the vegetables just until they start to brown, then return all the meat to the pot, resting it on top of the vegetables. Add the ham stock. Add water if necessary to bring the level of liquid halfway up the sides of the meat.

Cover the pot, place in the middle of the oven, and cook for 1 1/2 hours or until the meat is very tender. Then remove the pot from the oven and allow the meat to cool in its broth (you can eat the pork now, but it will be much better after it's had time to sit in the broth for a night in the refrigerator).

When the braise has cooled overnight, use a spoon to scrape off any congealed fat on the top of the broth. (There will probably be quite a bit. If you save it you can use it as a very flavorful cooking medium for future dishes.) Allow the stew to warm up enough that you can remove the meat from the broth without tearing it. Pour the liquid and vegetables through a food mill or into a food processor to puree, then recombine the puree and liquid with the meat. Heat through on the stovetop, check for seasoning, and serve with grits (page 56).

sausage

yields two 16-inch rolls; six 4 1/4-inch slices each roll

Making your own breakfast sausage takes a little more work than slicing off the end of a tube of grocery store sausage, but if you don't have a great butcher shop nearby, this may be your best chance at getting fresh, delicious sausage.

You will need one piece of specialized equipment to make sausage: a meat grinder. If you have a good stand mixer, like the KitchenAid, you can buy it as an attachment. It's worth getting: in addition to enabling you to make your own sausage (and scrapple), it lets you grind your own meat for hamburgers—and once you've done that you'll never go back.

The section of Brooklyn where Egg is was solidly Italian until a decade or so ago, and that legacy inspired the seasoning in our breakfast mix. You can adjust the seasonings as you like, adding sweet spices or toning down the red pepper flakes—just keep the amount of salt the same and you can't really go wrong.

5 lb pork shoulder or Boston butt, fat intact

1 1/2 tbsp (1 1/2 oz) kosher salt

1 tbsp red pepper flakes

2 tsp black pepper

1 1/2 tbsp fennel seed

scant 2 tbsp apple cider vinegar

Cut pork shoulder into 1- or 1 1/2-inch chunks (small enough to fit easily down the feed tube of your meat grinder). Add salt, red pepper flakes, black pepper, and fennel seed and combine thoroughly. Rub the spices into the meat.

Refrigerate the seasoned meat overnight if you can, or for at least an hour—the longer you let it sit, the better the spices will meld. Your main goal here is to get the meat thoroughly cold before you grind it.

When you're ready to grind, set a bowl to catch the sausage as it comes out. Use a coarse grind plate if you have the option. Make sure all the connections in your grinder are tight—the plate screwed on tight to the end of the tube, the tube clamped tight to the motor.

Feed the cold, seasoned meat into the grinder, pressing gently with a plunger as necessary to keep the meat moving through. Don't force it, though—the meat should come through looking ground but not pasty.

>>

Once all the meat has been ground, put it in the fridge for 15 minutes or so to cool again before the next step. Set up your mixer with a bowl and paddle. Add the chilled meat in one-pound batches to the mixer bowl and mix on low speed for 30 seconds, or until you see the meat starting to cling together (you're basically gently kneading the meat, developing a protein that will help bind the meat together). Add a splash of vinegar (no more than a teaspoon per pound) and mix until it's incorporated with the meat, then remove the mixed sausage to a separate bowl and hold in the refrigerator while you mix the next batch.

When you've mixed all the meat, pack it together into a ball. Spread 2 2-foot-long pieces of plastic wrap or foil on your counter and divide the meat evenly between them. For each piece of wrap, form a cylinder of sausage longwise down the middle of it. Wrap the long sides of the wrap around the sausage, roll it against the countertop, and twist the ends like a piece of candy until the plastic is tight against the meat and the meat is in a neat roll. You can freeze one and refrigerate the other. Slicing pieces of meat as you need them is much easier if the sausage is well chilled.

To cook, cut a 1/4-inch slice off the roll with a very sharp knife. Add it to a hot skillet lightly oiled with bacon fat or vegetable oil—you won't need much as the sausage is fatty enough to lubricate itself. Cook 2 minutes undisturbed, turn and cook for 2 1/2 minutes more. Check the sausage frequently as you cook it by making a tiny slit in the top with a sharp paring knife. You want it cooked through, but only just.

scrapple

makes 4 bricks, each serve 12

"What is scrapple, exactly?" That's the toughest question any Egg server gets. If you describe it by listing its ingredients, you lose folks at "liver" or "heart." We tell people it's like sausage bound with cornmeal, and sometimes that gets them. But people who know scrapple get so excited when they see it on the menu that it makes up for all the customers too squeamish to take the plunge.

Scrapple's not simple to make, but it freezes well, so you can make a batch and have enough to last you weeks or months. As with sausage (page 117), you'll need a meat grinder (or a meat-grinder attachment) for this recipe.

1/4 lb pork heart

1 lb pork liver

2 cups milk

2 lb pork shoulder, cut into cubes

1 shy cup unbleached flour

1 1/2 cups cornmeal

1/4 cup kosher salt

1 1/2 tbsp black pepper

1/2 tsp cayenne pepper

1/2 tsp nutmeg

1 large or 1 1/2 medium onions, cut in a small dice

2 tsp oil or bacon fat

3 1/2 cups country ham stock page 108

2 tsp fresh sage, minced

Clean the pork offal (the heart and liver), cut into cubes, and soak in milk in the refrigerator for at least an hour or overnight.

Store the cubed pork shoulder in the refrigerator with the offal while you measure the remaining ingredients. Combine the flour, cornmeal, salt, peppers, and nutmeg with a whisk until well-blended.

When the meat and the offal are thoroughly chilled, drain the milk, run them through your meat grinder, and set aside. Heat fat or oil in a wide pot or dutch oven. Cook the onions over low heat until they are very soft and translucent, about 20 minutes, then add the stock. When the stock comes to a simmer, add the ground pork shoulder and offal, mixing it in with a whisk or a large slotted spoon so that it's evenly distributed. Add the cornmeal-flour-seasoning mixture, and cook on low heat for about 50 minutes, stirring often. You will know that it is thick enough to stop when you drag a spatula through the center of the pot and the mixture holds its place instead of pooling back into the center. Stir in the sage and remove from heat.

>>

Spread the mixture into a parchment- or plastic wrap—lined 9x13-inch pan and chill overnight. The following day, portion into long bricks, cutting crosswise into 4 pieces. Wrap tightly and freeze any that you won't use in short order.

To cook, slice into 1/3- or 1/2-inch thick pieces and fry in a little bacon fat or vegetable oil. Allow each piece to cook undisturbed in the pan for 2–3 minutes until it's crispy and dark brown. Flip it carefully with a spatula and cook until the second side is also crispy. Serve with eggs and hot sauce.

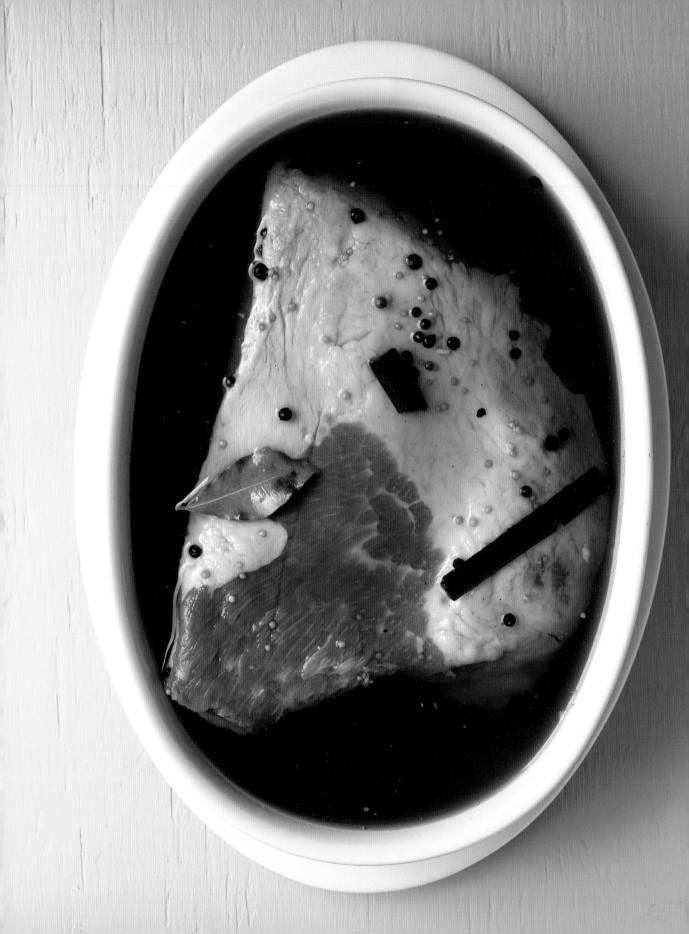

corned beef

Making your own corned beef or lamb is a project, no question—but it's well worth the trouble if you want to have the most delicious red flannel hash (page 50) you ever tried. This recipe can be easily halved if you don't want to cook as much meat, but corned beef freezes well, too, so you can cook and portion it, stick it in the freezer, and have corned beef on hand for weeks to come.

1 piece beef brisket, 6–8 lb

FOR BRINE

3 quart water may use 2 quart water and 1 quart ice to cool quickly

2 cups dark beer stout or porter is best; avoid hoppy beers like IPAs

2 cups kosher salt

1/2 cups turbinado sugar

1 1/2 tbsp curing salt

1/2 cinnamon stick

2 tsp mustard seeds

2 tsp black peppercorns

3 whole cloves

8 whole allspice berries

12 whole juniper berries

2 bay leaves

TO COOK

1 small onion, quartered

1 large carrot or parsnip, roughly chopped

1 stalk celery, roughly chopped

1/2 head of garlic, crushed

Place water into a large stockpot with spices. Bring to a boil and add beer. Remove from heat and cool (if using ice, start with 2 quarts of water, then add 1 quart of ice to cool brine after it has boiled). Once cool, place the meat in a container and cover with brine. Weight down with a plate to keep meat submerged. Refrigerate for 8–10 days, making sure meat is always covered.

After brine period, remove meat from the brine and rinse. Place the meat into a pot just large enough to hold it, add the onion, carrot, and celery, and cover with water by 1 inch. Set over high heat and bring to a boil. Reduce the heat to low, cover, and simmer very gently for 3 hours or until the meat is fork tender, but not falling apart. Alternatively, put the meat, water, and vegetables in a deep baking dish, cover with foil, and cook in the oven at 300°F for 3 hours. Cool the meat in the liquid for an hour or overnight. Thinly slice across the grain for sandwiches, or cube for use in hashes.

steak and eggs

1 – 1 1/2 lb steak, cut thick

1 tbsp kosher salt

3 tbsp butter

1 tbsp vegetable oil

2 tsp crushed black pepper

8 eggs, cooked as you like them

Steak and eggs is one of the few remaining dishes in the American breakfast canon that reflects what people used to consider for their morning meal. You can make a passable version of it with the leftover meat from your previous night's meal, but if you want to do it right, you should cook your steak with all the affection and attention you'd give it if you were cooking for a fancy dinner.

This is a stovetop recipe for steak, and it's not shy about fat. Fat is the best way to get a good sear on your meat indoors. You may want to put a shower cap over your smoke detectors before you start this one, or you may just want to let the smoke detectors serve as the alarm clock for the rest of the house. When your family finds this at the table waiting for them, they may forgive you for the rude awakening.

Wash and dry your steak before seasoning it generously with kosher salt on both sides—don't hold back.

Heat the butter and oil in a skillet over medium-high heat. Once the butter is melted and its foam has subsided, pat the steak dry one more time before laying it carefully in the butter and oil, taking care not to splash it.

Allow the steak to cook undisturbed for 4–5 minutes before lifting an edge to check how it's browning. When the down side is well browned, flip the steak over and cook on the other side.

We like our steaks rare to medium-rare. Sometimes that means we only get one side well browned before we take it out of the pan, but better to have one good crust and tender meat than two good crusts around a piece of dried-out beef. If you keep your eye out for the first beads of red juice emerging through the side of the steak, about 3 minutes after you've flipped it, you can use them as your indication that it's time to pull the steak from heat (3 minutes for rare, 4 minutes for medium-rare).

Pepper the steak and allow it to sit for 7–10 minutes before you slice it.

Serve with eggs cooked in your preferred style and some parsley sauce (page 183) and hash browns (page 40) if you like.

steak and sunnyside up eggs (page 26)

fried chicken biscuit

serves 4

We've harbored a secret crush on a fried chicken biscuit made by our friends at Pies & Thighs—a great Southern restaurant just down the street from Egg. Our cooks do their best to replicate it for themselves whenever we have a piece of chicken to spare in the kitchen.

2 boneless, skinless chicken breasts, filleted or pounded flat and cut into 4 pieces

1 quart chicken brine page 128

1/3 cup vegetable oil

4 biscuits page 72

FOR THE BREADING

1 egg

1 cup heavy cream

hot sauce

3 cups white bread crumbs

FOR THE SAUCE

2 tbsp hot sauce

1/4 cup honey

Brine the chicken breast in chicken brine for 8–12 hours, but no longer.

Mix the egg well in a bowl, then add heavy cream and a few dashes of hot sauce. Remove the chicken from the brine and rinse or wipe off any spices clinging to it. Dredge the chicken in the cream/egg mixture, then roll in bread crumbs. Store on wax paper while you prepare the pan to cook them.

Heat vegetable oil in a pan just large enough to contain the chicken in one uncrowded layer. Heat over medium until the oil is 375°F, or until a corner of the chicken sizzles as soon as you dip it into the oil.

Gently lay the chicken pieces into the oil and allow to cook undisturbed for 3 minutes, or until the breading is golden brown. Flip the chicken to its other side and continue to cook another 3–4 minutes.

Remove the chicken to a paper towel and slice in half. (If any of the chicken still looks raw, return it to the pan to cook a minute longer, or place it in the oven at 350°F until it's fully cooked.)

Split the biscuits in two and heat them up in a toaster oven or oven. Stir together the hot sauce and the honey. Place the fried chicken on the biscuit and drizzle it with the honey hot sauce.

chicken brine

yields 3 quarts

1 cup kosher salt

1/3 cup turbinado sugar

1 clove

10 black peppercorns

5 allspice berries

1 tbsp coriander seeds

1 bay leaf

Bring all ingredients to a boil in 3 quarts of water. Remove from heat and taste—brine should be very salty. Allow to cool completely by storing it in the fridge overnight (if you make the brine extra salty you can cool it by putting ice directly in the brine). Once it's completely cool, pour enough of it over the chicken to submerge the meat completely to cover.

chicken and tomatillo stew

serves 6–8

Here's a good breakfast stew for summer. The bright flavors of tomatillos liven up the broth and wake up your tongue. Like most stews, this one benefits from resting for a night or more in the fridge after you cook it, so make it one afternoon to feed you at breakfast during the week. It's great over grits and is a great excuse to have a beer with breakfast.

2 poblano peppers

1 whole chicken, cut into parts

kosher salt

black pepper

vegetable oil, duck fat, or bacon fat

2 tsp coriander seed

8 tomatillos

1/2 medium onion, diced

1 medium carrot, diced

1 celery rib, diced

2 cloves garlic, minced

2 cups chicken stock

1 lime, quartered + more for garnish

6 cups cooked grits page 56

Roast the poblano peppers over the flame of your stove or under your broiler, turning often until the peppers are blackened on all sides. Then place them in a sealed container or plastic bag to steam and cool. When they're cool enough to handle, rub the charred skin off the peppers with your fingers or the back of a paring knife. Cut out the stems, split longwise down the side, and scrape out the seeds. Chop the roasted peppers into small ribbons.

Pat the chicken pieces dry and season with salt and pepper. Heat a tablespoon of fat (vegetable oil, duck fat, bacon fat) in a Dutch oven over medium-high heat. Sear the chicken, skin side down first, to get a nice crust on each piece, 7–8 minutes. (Leave the chicken in place while it cooks—resist the temptation to poke it and move it around!) You'll probably have to sear the pieces in two batches to avoid crowding the pan—it's worth it.

>>

chicken tomatillo stew with grits (page 56)

Turn pieces over and continue searing for another 5–6 minutes. Check the bottom of the pan to make sure the residue isn't burning or blackening. If you see it starting to burn in a spot, turn the heat down slightly and cover the burned spot by moving the chicken over the top of it—this'll cool the hot spot down and help loosen the stuck parts.

After you finish the first batch, set it on a sheet pan or large platter (skin side up!) while you cook the second batch.

While the chicken is searing, grind the coriander in a mortar or spice grinder. Husk, rinse, and halve the tomatillos.

When the chicken is all seared, place it on a pan or platter and pour off all but 1 tablespoon of fat from the pot. Put the onion, carrot, celery, and garlic in the pot and turn down the heat to medium. Add a teaspoon of salt and stir the vegetables frequently until they've released enough juice to loosen all the residue on the bottom of the pan. Continue cooking until soft, 5–6 minutes, adding a little water if necessary to keep any spots from burning.

Once the vegetables have softened, add the coriander and cook until it's aromatic. Add tomatillos and stock and simmer until the tomatillos have broken down, 15 minutes. Add chopped poblano peppers and a quartered lime to the pot, then gently lay the chicken parts, skin side up, on top of the stew.

Simmer for 20 minutes, or until chicken is tender. Season to taste with salt and pepper.

To serve, dish out grits into a shallow bowl and spoon stew over top. Top with a piece or two of chicken, a wedge of lime.

PRO TIP

If the number of people you're serving doesn't divide neatly into the pieces of chicken you've got, you can also pull the meat from the bone and return it to the stew.

duck confit

yields just shy of 3 cups

It's a great thing to have a container of confit in your fridge—you can heat up a little bit when you're having breakfast by yourself, and it's the kind of thing that'll blow minds when you trot it out for a breakfast with friends. It keeps a long time, so it's smart to make a lot of it to keep on hand. Use confit in our duck hash recipe, in dirty rice, or as a side meat with eggs, toast, and a simple salad.

It's best to confit duck in duck fat—you can usually buy it at a good butcher's shop. If you can't get it, you can get by with good olive oil, too.

FOR THE CURE

2 cups kosher salt

3/4 cup turbinado sugar

1 tsp coriander seeds

2 tsp whole black pepper

2 tsp fresh thyme

1 tsp chopped fresh rosemary

1 star anise

FOR THE DUCK

6 pieces each, leg and thigh

FOR COOKING

5 cloves garlic

4 star anise

4 bay leaves

1 quart duck fat or olive oil

To make the cure: Mix together the salt and sugar. Heat a small sauté pan and toast the spices and herbs over medium heat until they are aromatic. Then dump them into a mortar or onto a cutting board and crush them with a pestle or the broad side of a knife. Mix the spices with the salt and sugar mix.

To cure the duck: Pat dry and rub the legs and thighs all over with the cure, making sure to coat everything. Put some extra cure in the bottom of a glass dish that can hold all the duck legs and tuck the duck in on top. Spread more of the cure on top of the duck, or between each layer if you stack it more than one layer deep.

Cover the dish, place in the refrigerator, and cure the duck for 24 hours before rinsing off the spices and salt and patting the meat dry. The meat should have firmed up in the cure.

When ready to cook, preheat oven to 250ºF. Lay the meat in a heavy ovenproof pot large enough for duck to fit snugly in a single layer. Add the garlic, star anise, bay leaves, and the fat. Cover and place in the oven for 3 1/2–4 hours, or until the meat has started to shrink from the end of the bone and the fat is very aromatic. Remove the pot from the oven and allow to cool until you can handle it.

At this point, you can either shred the meat (which we do, so that it's easy to pick out for a quick breakfast; discard the bones or use them for stock) or lay it intact into a glass or ceramic dish. Pour the molten fat and aromatic herbs and spices over the duck and allow the meat to ripen another day or more before using.

fried oysters with scrambled eggs (page 20)
and Bloody Mary (page 194)

fried oysters

Oysters may not be the first thing you think of for breakfast, but once you've had them you'll want to start every sunny Saturday morning with a plate of oysters, scrambled eggs, some pickles, and a Bloody Mary.

serves 4

1 egg

1 cup heavy cream

hot sauce

24 oysters shucked + 2 tbsp liquor reserved

2 cups cornmeal

1 tbsp kosher salt

1 tsp black pepper

1/2 tsp cayenne pepper

1/3 cup vegetable oil, bacon fat, or combination

lemon slices for serving

Begin by making a wash for your oysters: Beat the egg with the heavy cream, hot sauce, and reserved oyster liquor.

Blend the cornmeal, salt, black pepper, and cayenne in a small bowl.

Heat the vegetable oil or bacon fat in a medium skillet, big enough to hold about half the oysters at once.

While the oil is heating, add the shucked oysters to the cream and egg wash. Then roll each oyster in the cornmeal and spice mixture. Use one hand to transfer the oyster to the cornmeal, shake the bowl to cover the oyster in meal, and then use your other hand to pick up the cornmeal-crusted oyster and slip it gently into the hot oil. Repeat until you have half the oysters in the pan.

Oysters cook quickly, and you don't want to cook them too long or they'll dry out. As soon as the cornmeal turns lightly golden on one side, turn the oyster over. You'll probably need to start turning the first oyster you put in the pan as soon as you put the twelfth oyster in. Once they've browned on the second side, remove to a paper towel or wire rack and cook the second half of the oysters. Serve with lemon.

smoked trout salad

Egg is just a few blocks from one of the best fish-smoking operations in the country, Acme Smoked Fish. If you eat smoked fish of any kind in New York City, there's a good chance it got smoked there. We visit on Friday mornings, when they open up the smokehouse to the public and people of every generation and every ethnic background line up down the block to buy their weekly supply of salmon, herring, whitefish, and trout. If you can't get smoked trout, any hot-smoked fish would do the job.

serves 4

1 lb fingerling potatoes or new potatoes clean, but skins on

2 sprigs fresh thyme

2 cloves of garlic

2 tbsp kosher salt

2 fillets or 8-oz package smoked trout, picked free of bones and flaked into small bite-size pieces

1/2–3/4 cup mustard-caraway vinaigrette page 190

16 cups (1/2 lb) mixed salad greens

4 medium-boiled eggs, peeled page 31

sea salt

Put the potatoes, thyme, garlic, and salt in a pot and cover with cold water. Bring to a boil, then cook at a gentle boil for 10–15 minutes, until tender and easy to pierce with the end of a paring knife. Drain and let cool, then cut into bite-size pieces.

In a large bowl, toss the smoked trout and potatoes together with 1/2 cup of the dressing. Add the mixed greens, toss together, and dress a bit more, to your taste. With a sharp knife, cut the eggs lengthwise in half or into quarters. Plate the salad, trying to get a good balance of all the ingredients on each plate, and put egg slices on top of each. Add a pinch of sea salt and serve.

vegetables and a little fruit

No one thinks twice about eating fruit for breakfast. You wouldn't ordinarily sit down for a dinner of berries and melon, but people do it first thing in the morning all the time. It makes sense: After a long sleep, your body craves quick energy, and fruit is an easy (and fairly nutritious) sugar, which gives you the jolt you need. It's less common that people wake up and make themselves a bowl of vegetables. A mess of quickly sautéed snap peas or a few slices of tomato at the height of summer make great morning dishes, but for some reason we've talked ourselves out of thinking we want them at that hour.

But you do want them: Adding vegetables to your morning menu opens you up to a world of possibility, especially in winter, when good fruit is hard to find. You can't get much but apples for most of the winter in New York, but there's a variety of squashes and potatoes and hearty greens from the first day of fall to the day strawberries start arriving at the greenmarkets again in the spring.

We serve more vegetables than we do fruit at Egg. Most of the time, it's simply sautéed kale, which we offer as our vegetarian alternative to country ham, bacon, or sausage. But we also serve sides of other vegetables in season—asparagus, peas, dandelion greens, squash, ramps, tomatoes, mushrooms, and beans. And they go down easily by themselves or paired with eggs, hash, meats, or grains. You just have to adjust your perspective a few degrees.

sautéed kale

serves 2–4

If anything's proved to us that people are open to change at breakfast, it's been the popularity of kale as a side dish. We've gone through a case of kale every day since 2009 when we settled on it as our standard vegetarian side dish for people who didn't want bacon or sausage with their eggs. We tried just about everything else—from mushrooms to vegetarian sausage—and we still offer other vegetables in season. But nothing was ever as popular as our kale, and because it's delicious and easy to get year-round, even in New York, we were happy to keep serving it. We offer it as a side for omelets, grits, and eggs, and the Eggs Rothko (page 36). We also have plenty of customers who just order huge bowls of it.

Because this preparation is so simple, make sure your kale is good to start with. Buy at a farmers' market, get an organic variety, or grow it yourself if you can. Lacinato, Tuscan, dinosaur, or red or white Russian are all good varieties.

1 clove garlic, minced

1/2 (3 tbsp) shallot, minced

1 tbsp olive oil

4 cups coarsely chopped kale, thick stems removed

kosher salt

black pepper

pinch red pepper flakes

lemon juice or white wine optional

In a large (10-inch) deep skillet, sauté garlic and shallot in olive oil until the shallot is translucent, 2–3 minutes. Put the kale in the pan along with a pinch of salt, a grinding of pepper, and a pinch of red pepper flakes.

How long you cook the kale depends on which type it is. If your kale is very thick, as it is at the end of winter, you'll need to cook it longer; if it's young and tender, a flash in the pan will do it. Just test it as you cook to get it to the point of tenderness you like. When kale is nearly done, add a splash of white wine or some lemon, if using—this will brighten up the dish.

PRO TIP

Adding a splash of water to the kale as you cook it will help tenderize and steam it and prevent it from scorching.

Sautéed kale with Eggs Rothko (page 36) and
broiled tomatoes (page 143)

broiled tomatoes

serves 3–4 as a side

I was often sent from the table for refusing to eat my mother's broiled tomatoes when I was a kid. They're a traditional Southern dish: sugared until they're blindingly sweet, stewed almost to a pulp, mixed in with shredded bread, and blackened in the broiler. They were served as a kind of condiment—good with roast meats, in particular.

These tomatoes are a lot less sweet than my family's version (which I've since come to love). They're incredibly simple but surprisingly satisfying and versatile. We serve them to brighten up a plate of eggs or with any rich, buttery dish, like Eggs Rothko (page 36).

1 28-oz can whole peeled tomatoes

5 tbsp minced onion

2 tbsp olive oil

2 tsp turbinado sugar

1 tsp kosher salt

1 tsp black pepper

Drain the tomatoes. Slice them lengthwise into crescent-shaped sections, reserving their juices (yield about 1/2 cup juice). Discard any large pieces of skin or stem.

In an ovenproof sauté pan or shallow skillet, sweat the onion in olive oil over low-medium heat until translucent, about 5 minutes.

Add the tomatoes and strained juices to the onions and olive oil, then add sugar, salt, and black pepper.

Gently simmer the tomatoes for 20 minutes, or until most of the juice has cooked down and the tomatoes are tender.

While the tomatoes are simmering, preheat the broiler.

Slide pan under broiler for 3–4 minutes so tomatoes partially blacken. Remove the pan, stir tomatoes, and return to the broiler to partially blacken again. Serve hot.

These tomatoes will keep in a jar in your fridge for 3–5 days. Reheat before serving.

carrot yogurt salad

We first made this dish for elementary schoolchildren at an event we do with Wellness in the Schools, an organization that fights for better food in New York City's public school system. I wasn't sure kids would be into roasted carrots and yogurt so early in the day, but they loved it—one even had his teacher email us for the recipe. If it's good in a raucous elementary school cafeteria, it's even better in the comfort of home.

serves 4–6

4 large (1 lb) whole raw carrots

1 tbsp olive oil

kosher salt

black pepper

1 cup plain whole-milk yogurt not "Greek-style"

1 clove garlic, minced

1 tsp lemon juice

2 tsp coriander seed, crushed, or coriander powder

1 sprig flat-leaf parsley, leaves removed

minced cilantro optional

Preheat oven to 450°F.

Cut the carrots into rounds or wedges by slicing diagonally across the carrot. Put carrots in a bowl with olive oil, a pinch of salt, and some pepper. Toss until the carrots are well-coated with oil and seasoning.

Pour the carrots out onto a baking sheet and spread out into a thin layer, then roast for 20–23 minutes or until soft and browned at the edges (keep an eye on them as they cook and stir if some start to get too brown).

Once the carrots have cooked, allow them to cool completely.

Put the carrots in a clean bowl and add yogurt a few tablespoons at a time, stirring, until the carrot slices are well coated with yogurt. Add the garlic to the bowl, along with the lemon juice and the coriander.

Add parsley and stir to combine. Allow the salad to sit for an hour at room temperature or longer in the refrigerator so the ingredients can mingle and meld. Serve with cilantro if you like.

collard greens

Collards are an intense dish for breakfast, but served in their broth with a little hot sauce over a crumbled-up biscuit, they're an excellent and simple way to start a day. And they're a great use of a leftover ham hock when you have one.

4 strips bacon

1/2 large yellow onion, diced

1 clove garlic, minced

2 bunches (2 lb) collard greens, center ribs removed, cut into 1-inch ribbons crosswise

a country ham bone or ham hock
or use country ham stock (page 108) in place of water for cooking

2 tbsp apple cider vinegar

1 tbsp molasses

1 tbsp turbinado sugar

kosher salt

black pepper

red pepper flakes

Cut bacon into small strips and heat over medium heat in a stock pot until bacon is crisp and most of the fat is rendered. Remove the bacon and reserve, leaving the fat in the pot.

Add the onion to the bacon fat in the pot and cook over medium-low heat until it is lightly browned, about 8 minutes, then add the garlic and cook another minute.

Add chopped collards, ham bone, vinegar, molasses, and enough water to make the leaves float freely, 1 1/2–2 quarts (the leaves may rise up above the level of the water at first, but as they cook they'll reduce significantly in volume). Add the sugar, a healthy pinch each of salt and pepper, and red pepper flakes to taste.

Bring to a simmer and cook for 45 minutes or until the collards are tender and the broth is rich and fragrant.

simple roasted potatoes

serves 4–6

1 1/2 lb fingerling potatoes

1/4 cup olive oil

black pepper

kosher salt

2 cloves garlic optional

Roasted potatoes are an area where you have an advantage over a restaurant cook—they take a little too long to cook to order, and they don't hold well.

To get your potatoes right, cut them into even-sized pieces (we like to cut them at odd angles to keep them interesting) and use a generous amount of oil. Salt them liberally after cooking. We sometimes put a few cloves of smashed garlic in the pan with our potatoes to add an additional hint of flavor, though one of the things you'll discover if you use good potatoes is that they have a lot of interesting flavor on their own!

Preheat oven to 450°F. Cut potatoes into roughly equal-size pieces. Toss in a bowl with the olive oil and some black pepper, then spread potatoes out on a cookie sheet.

Go through the potatoes and make sure you've got the cut sides in contact with the bottom of the pan—they'll crisp up best that way. Put a few pieces of gently smashed garlic in the oil, too, if you like.

Roast potatoes for 15 minutes without stirring—then use a spatula to move a couple around on the pan. If they're well-browned, carry on mixing them all up a bit; if they're not browned yet, leave the rest of the potatoes alone (different kinds of potatoes have different sugar and moisture contents, so they'll brown at different rates).

Check potatoes again after another 10 minutes (25 minutes in all). If they're well browned and a fork goes easily through one, they're done. Pull them out, season generously with salt, and serve sooner than later. Don't pile them into a bowl or cover the pan—the potatoes will steam and lose their crispness.

spring peas with country ham

serves 4 as a side

This is as simple a recipe as you could dream up, but it shows off the incredible depth and versatility of country ham. We use spring peas—snap or snow peas, for example—but you could make it with any number of vegetables. Delicate green beans, young asparagus, or even fiddleheads could all work, too.

1 tbsp oil or fat

2 tbsp minced country ham page 100

1 1/2 cups sugar snap peas in their shells, trimmed

kosher salt

black pepper

Heat the fat in a sauté pan over medium heat. Add country ham and cook gently until the ham's fat is translucent and the pieces of ham have just started to crisp at the edges, about 3 minutes. Add the peas and toss to coat them with the fat and ham.

Cook over medium heat until the peas are bright green but still have a little crunch, about 3 minutes more. Season to taste with salt and pepper. Remove from heat and serve.

sautéed apples

We always offer one side of seasonal fruit at Egg. In the spring, we serve strawberries and blueberries; as summer heats up we turn to peaches and apricots. But for the long, long months of winter, it's mostly apples. Sometimes we'll find something to do with cranberries; sometimes we'll find pears or quince, but for most of the cold months between November and May, we serve a lot of apples.

This recipe works best with tart, crisp apples like Galas or Fujis. We'll often add a little lemon juice to the pan to brighten up the flavor at the end.

serves 2

1/2 tbsp butter for cooking + 1/2 tbsp to finish

1 apple, cored and sliced into 1/2-inch thick wedges

2 tsp turbinado sugar

1 tsp fresh lemon juice optional

Heat a medium (10- or 12-inch) sauté pan over medium-high heat. Add 1/2 tablespoon of butter. Once it has melted and bubbled up, add the apple slices all at once. Using your fingers or tongs, turn all of the apple slices so that they are cut-side down in the pan in a single layer. Sprinkle the sugar over the apples and shake the pan to distribute it among the slices. If the apples are very dry and have not released any juice, you may need to add a splash of water or a squeeze of lemon juice to keep the sugar from burning.

Turn the apples once they have browned nicely on the first side, 2–4 minutes. As soon as the apples seem soft, another 3–4 minutes, pull the pan off heat. Add the remaining 1/2 tablespoon of butter and 1 teaspoon lemon juice (if using). Swirl the pan around to emulsify the butter with the lemon juice and serve.

seared mushrooms

These simple mushrooms are a great complement to eggs—and they are the foundation for the vegetarian version of our biscuits and gravy.

serves 1

2 cups (6 oz) cremini mushrooms

1 1/2 tbsp vegetable oil

kosher salt

black pepper

1 clove garlic, minced

1 tsp thyme fresh or dried

Trim and cut the mushrooms by cutting off any dried-out or brown ends of the stems, then cut the mushrooms into wedges (cutting them into slightly odd pieces makes them a little prettier and more fun to eat).

Heat the oil in a sauté pan wide enough to hold the mushrooms without crowding (there should be a little space between the pieces for the mushrooms' juices to cook off). Turn mushrooms so that their cut sides are down. Add salt and pepper and allow to cook over medium-high heat undisturbed for 2–3 minutes, or until the mushrooms have browned nicely on one side. Reduce heat to medium (so garlic won't burn) and stir in the garlic and the thyme, and cook another minute or two until the garlic is tender and fragrant and the mushrooms are browned and tender. Remove from heat and serve (or use in the recipe for vegetarian gravy on page 46).

sage-roasted squash

serves 2–4, depending on the size of the squash

Squash is one of the foods that make us look forward to summer's end—once the corn and tomatoes are gone, and the lettuce greens are retreating to the greenhouse, squash is just coming into its own. Sweet, plentiful, and easy, it's a great breakfast vegetable—serve it alongside grits and bacon for a perfect autumnal morning.

1 large or 2 small winter squash butternut, acorn, or kabocha

1/4 cup vegetable or olive oil

kosher salt

black pepper

5–6 large leaves sage, cut into thin ribbons

Preheat oven to 425°F.

With a very sharp knife, square off the ends of the squash—slice off the stem and flower ends. Then use a vegetable peeler to cut off all the skin on the squash. (If you're trimming a creased squash like an acorn, you may find it easier to cut the squash into slices along the creases before peeling.)

Cut the squash in half across to expose the seeds and use a spoon to scrape out the seeds and all the stringy tissue in the seed cavity

Cut the peeled squash into 1/2-inch cubes. Put the cubes in a bowl with 1/4 cup of oil and toss to coat. Add more oil if necessary—you want to make sure the squash is coated on all sides.

Spread the squash on a baking sheet in one layer and season with salt and black pepper. Roast for 20 minutes, then check to see if the bottoms of the squash are browning. If so, stir the sage into the squash and continue roasting until the squash is soft, about 5 minutes more.

PRO TIP

Take the seeds from the squash, clean them, and toast on a baking sheet in a 300°F oven with oil and salt. They're great on their own or tossed over a bowl of savory oatmeal.

---

beans and greens

serves 6

This is one of our favorite hearty vegetarian breakfasts—when we forgo the bacon fat. The rich flavor of onions sautéed dark over high heat makes the beans robust.

FOR THE BEANS

1 tbsp vegetable oil or bacon fat

1 small onion, diced

2 cloves garlic, chopped

2 cups Sea Island red peas or any other small, dried bean

kosher salt

FOR THE KALE

1/4 cup olive oil

1 onion, julienned

1 clove of garlic, chopped

2 cups canned or fresh whole tomatoes, chopped, 1 cup juice reserved

1/2 cup white wine

2 bunches (about 1 1/4 lb) of organic kale, thick stems removed, roughly chopped

a pinch of red pepper flakes

black pepper

To cook the beans, heat the oil or fat in a pot large enough to hold the beans. Cook the onion over medium-high heat, stirring frequently, until it is dark brown but not burned. Add the garlic for a minute, still stirring, then add the beans and enough water to cover them by 2–3 inches. Bring them to a boil then reduce heat and simmer for 1–3 hours until they are tender and have no hint of chalkiness within. (The length of cooking will depend on the type of bean you're using.) When the beans are tender, add salt and set aside.

Heat oil in a deep pot over medium-low heat, then add onions. Cook together until the onions are nicely caramelized, about 10 minutes. Add the garlic and cook for one minute. Add the chopped tomatoes and juice, wine, and 2 cups of water. Add the kale. Season with pepper flakes, salt, and pepper and simmer over medium-low heat until the kale is tender (about 20 minutes unless it's late in the season and your kale is thick).

Serve the beans, drained, with the greens in a bowl over grits (page 56), cornbread (page 80), or with a biscuit (page 72), if you like.

beans and greens with cornbread (page 80)

spiced pecans

yields 1 quart of spiced pecans

These simple roasted nuts are delicious in a salad, like the farro salad on page 68, and they're an easy (if addictive) breakfast on their own. This recipe makes a lot, but you'll be sorry if you make any less.

1 quart whole pecan halves

2 1/2 tbsp neutral oil such as canola or grapeseed

1 1/4 tsp fennel seed, lightly crushed

3/4 tsp red pepper flakes

1 1/2 tsp kosher salt

1/3 tsp black pepper

1/4 cup honey

Preheat oven to 400°F.

Toss nuts in oil to coat, then add fennel seed, pepper flakes, salt, and pepper. Line a baking sheet with parchment paper, then spread the nuts in one layer on the baking sheet and roast to a golden brown. Be careful not to burn as the nuts will become very bitter. Remove from oven and drizzle with honey while still hot.

Allow nuts to cool before storing in airtight containers.

cornbread and tomato salad

serves 6–8

This is kind of a riff on a classic panzanella, made with skillet cornbread and the best tomatoes you can get your hands on. It's a great way to show off a variety of heirloom and specialty tomatoes. It's also a great way to use any extra cornbread you may have left after making the recipe on page 80. If you can get your hands on bush basil—a tiny and delicious variety—substitute this for standard basil. As the salad sits it'll get more and more delicious as the tomato juices mingle and soak into the cornbread.

1/2 recipe cornbread page 80

3 lb assorted tomatoes

kosher salt

black pepper

1 leek

2 tbsp olive oil

3 ears corn

2 tsp apple cider or white wine vinegar

1/8 cup picked basil leaves

Preheat oven to 350°F. Cut the cornbread into bite-size pieces and spread on a baking sheet. Bake until bread is just crispy on the corners around 15 minutes.

Cut the tomatoes into pieces you can eat in a single bite and place in a bowl. Add a teaspoon of salt and a few grindings of black pepper and allow the tomatoes to marinate in their juices.

Trim the tops and root end of the leek and split it in half lengthwise. Wash out any dirt that's hiding between the layers of the leek and then slice it crosswise into thin ribbons. Heat 2 teaspoons of olive oil in a small sauté pan and cook the leeks very gently until they are completely soft but not brown.

One at a time, stand the ears of corn on the fatter end and carefully slice the kernels off with a sharp knife. Heat another sauté pan with a teaspoon of oil. When the pan is very hot, throw the corn kernels in and sear them. Be careful—they may jump and spit. When you've managed to get a bit of sear on half of the kernels, call it a day and remove from heat.

Shortly before serving, combine the cornbread, leeks, and corn with the tomatoes and mix gently (your hands are the best tool for this). Depending on the acidity and juiciness of your tomatoes, you may have all the dressing you need right there from the tomatoes' juices. If not, add a splash each of olive oil and apple cider or white wine vinegar. Just before serving, add the basil leaves, tearing them if they are large.

stewed summer beans

serves 4

These beans are good any time of day: You can make them as a side for your dinner and keep the leftovers to reheat with a plate of duck hash in the morning. They're cooked in an old-school Southern style, until they're tender and flavorful—a distinct difference from the general taste for crisp and barely cooked beans.

3/4 cup sliced leeks

2 tbsp olive oil

1 small clove garlic

1 tbsp white wine

1 1/2 cups canned whole tomatoes, drained and chopped

1 lb string beans

1/4 tsp kosher salt

Cook leeks in oil and garlic until lightly colored. Add white wine, tomatoes, beans, and salt. Partially cover and simmer until beans are very tender, about 30–40 minutes.

Serve right away, or cool the beans in their broth and reheat later. (If you plan to eat them later, take them off heat before they're completely tender.)

caramelized grapefruit

serves 4

The tart shock of a grapefruit is beautifully mellowed by some caramelized turbinado sugar in this light morning dish. Fresh herbs are added at the end so that the heat of the sugar releases their aromas.

2 large grapefruits

1 tbsp + 1 tsp turbinado sugar

1 tsp chopped fresh mint or tarragon

Preheat the broiler of your oven or toaster oven.

Place each grapefruit on its side and slice in half, exposing a cross-section of segments. Use a paring knife to precut the grapefruit segments from above, slipping the knife, tip first, into each segment of the grapefruit right alongside the membrane. Sprinkle the sugar over the top of each fruit and slide the fruit under the broiler—the top of the fruit should be close to the flame or heating element. Cook until the sugar is melted and the edges of the grapefruit are blackened, about 2–3 minutes. Remove from the broiler and dress each with the chopped herbs while the grapefruits are still hot. Serve immediately.

peach and elderberry crumble

yields 1 9x13-inch crumble (serves 10–12)

For a short stretch during the summer, we can get peak-season stone fruit and berries at the same time. They make a nice combination, and a crumble is a great way to eat them together. (If you can't get elderberries, blackberries make a good substitute. You can use blackberry or elderberry jam.) Crumble keeps well in the fridge, so you can heat up pieces for breakfast as you need them. Try it with a little plain yogurt on the side, or with unsweetened whipped cream.

FOR THE FILLING

5 large peaches, sliced about 4 quarts

2 cups elderberries plus 3/4 cup white sugar
or 1 cup elderberry jam

2 tbsp maple sugar or turbinado sugar

2 tbsp all-purpose flour

1 tsp freshly grated nutmeg

1/4 tsp kosher salt

zest and juice of 1 lemon

FOR THE CRUMBLE

1 cup all-purpose flour

1/2 cup nuts, ground to a coarse meal in a food processor
almonds, walnuts, hazelnuts, and pecans all work well

1/2 cup white sugar

1/4 cup maple sugar or turbinado sugar

1/2 tsp ground cinnamon

1/2 tsp kosher salt

1 egg

10 tbsp butter, melted and slightly cooled

Preheat the oven to 350°F.

In a large bowl, toss all filling ingredients together and pour into a 9x13-inch baking dish.

Mix all crumble ingredients together, adding the slightly cooled melted butter last, and cover the filling with the crumble topping. Bake for 45 minutes until the filling is oozy and thick and the crumble topping is browned and crisp.

CLUES ACROSS
1. Coneless craters
6. Pullulate
10. Six (Spanish
14. Cricket
15. Deli
17.

parsnip and apple cider soup

serves 6

Why don't we eat more soup for break-fast? It's a perfect food for mornings: easy to reheat, comforting, delicious. This soup is easy to make and perfect on a cool fall morning, especially after a frost or two has made parsnips especially sweet.

4 tbsp (1/2 stick) butter

1/2 cup chopped leek white & light green parts only

9 medium parsnips (2 lb), peeled and roughly chopped

2 medium or 1 large (3/4 lb) russet potatoes

2 cups cream

2 quart water

1 1/2 cups apple cider

kosher salt

black pepper

In a large soup pot over medium heat, cook butter and leeks for 3 minutes until soft. Add the parsnips and potatoes and cover with the cream and water. Bring the soup to a simmer and continue cooking until all the parsnips and potatoes are tender, about 25 minutes. Add the apple cider and season with salt. Remove from the heat and allow soup to cool slightly before pureeing with an immersion blender or in a blender or food processor. Taste and adjust for salt. Pour it through a strainer for an especially velvety texture. Serve with a sprinkle of black pepper on top.

pickled ramps

yields 1 quart, give or take

Ramps are one of the few vegetables that we're still limited to eating fresh in one season of the year. You may not get great tomatoes in March or good butternut squash in June, but it's at least possible to get something. Not so with ramps, which come and go in a matter of weeks every spring, inducing a frenzy of people eager to eat as many as possible.

You can stretch out your enjoyment by preserving some of your haul as pickles. They're a beautiful thing to serve with some roasted or braised meats in the fall, or sliced onto scrambled eggs any time of year.

2 cups red wine vinegar

1/2 cup water

1/4 cup turbinado sugar

1 tsp kosher salt

1/2 tsp black pepper

15–20 ramps, floppy part of leaf and small roots trimmed

Combine all ingredients except the ramps in a deep pot and bring to a boil. While you're waiting for them to boil, prepare an ice bath: fill a bowl with ice cubes and just enough water to allow the ice to float.

When the pickling liquid is boiling, plunge the ramps into it and make sure they're fully submerged. Cook for 15–20 seconds, then pull them out gently with tongs or a small strainer and plunge them into the ice bath. Allow to sit a few minutes until completely cool, then drain well.

Allow the pickling liquid to cool completely, then add it to a jar with the blanched ramps. Store in the refrigerator and eat at your leisure—they will keep for at least six months.

lima bean salad

serves 4–6 as a side

We developed this dish when we were looking for a lighter alternative to collard greens to serve as a side with fried chicken. It's simple and good, and would make an excellent side in a picnic brunch with some deviled eggs (page 35).

1 cup dried lima beans you can use either the large or small variety

kosher salt

1 large stalk celery

2 tbsp pickled red onion page 177

1 tbsp sambal olek a common Vietnamese chili paste

black pepper

1/4 cup apple cider vinegar

Soak the beans in cold water overnight or for a couple of hours in just-boiled water. Drain off soaking liquid. Place beans in a medium-large saucepan. Add enough water to cover by 2 inches. Bring to a gentle boil over medium-high heat. Adjust heat so the beans cook at a very gentle simmer until they are just tender (begin checking after 15 minutes for baby limas, 20 minutes for large). Be careful to cook them gently so that they don't burst and fall apart (some of them will, but cooking gently will minimize your losses). The salad is cold, so leave time to cool the beans.

When the beans are cooked, add a teaspoon of salt and allow them to cool in their broth.

To assemble the salad, cut the celery in thin lunettes up the stalk—make each slice no more than 1/8-inch thick. Chop the pickled red onion and toss both the celery and onion into a bowl with the drained lima beans. Add the sambal olek and stir to mix everything together. Add a few grindings of pepper.

Add vinegar a tablespoon at a time, tasting as you go—stop when the salad is as tangy as you want it.

lima bean salad with cornbread (page 80) and
pickled eggs (page 32)

marinated beets

serves 4–6 as a side dish

The first thing we grew successfully at our little farm in the Catskills was a bumper crop of beets. We didn't know enough to plant them for succession harvests, so four 25-foot-long rows of beets came ripe at once. We learned to love them quite quickly after that, though we also learned how to plant smarter. This simple preparation makes for an easy side dish, but it's also an essential part of making Red Flannel Hash (page 50).

2–3 medium-sized beets (about 1 lb)

3 tbsp olive oil + 1 tbsp for roasting

kosher salt

black pepper

1 tbsp apple cider vinegar

1 tbsp thyme, tarragon, or parsley, chopped

Preheat the oven to 350°F.

Wash and trim the leaf ends of the beets. Place them in the middle of a large sheet of aluminum foil. Rub them with a tablespoon of olive oil, sprinkle with salt and pepper, and wrap them snugly in the foil. Put the package of beets in the oven and roast for 50–75 minutes (depending on the size of the beets), or until a sharp paring knife easily pierces them to the center.

Remove the beets from the oven and rest until they're cool enough to touch, then peel them using your fingers or a paring knife (they should peel quite easily). Cut them into 1-inch chunks, or bite-size pieces.

Make a quick marinade by whisking together the remaining olive oil, vinegar, and herbs. Add salt and pepper to taste, then add to a bowl with the beets and store until you're ready to use them.

sauces, spreads, jams, and relishes

The secret of a good cook is a pantry stocked with great condiments. If you've got a good stock of sauces and relishes to bring out with your meal, even a mundane entree can come alive—and that's as true at breakfast as any other meal. Try a splash of salsa verde on a scrambled egg sandwich, a couple tablespoons of pimento cheese stirred into grits, or some parsley sauce tucked under your breakfast steak.

salsa verde

yields 1 cup

This sauce is good with almost everything—we put it on chicken cutlets, chorizo, even French fries—but it's especially delicious with eggs. It's bright with acid and just spicy enough to wake up all the parts of you coffee can't get to. Tomatillos are delicious and versatile fruits, and they're well worth growing in your own garden, if you have one. They're prolific fruiters, and in our gardens we always find a few volunteers—plants that grow from seeds that fell from last season's crop—springing up where last year's crop stood.

7 medium (1 lb) tomatillos

2 cloves garlic, unpeeled

1 jalapeño pepper

1 bunch cilantro, cleaned and leaves picked from stems

juice of 1 lime

kosher salt

black pepper

Preheat the oven to 400ºF.

Remove the papery husks from the tomatillos and rinse them. Put the tomatillos, garlic, and jalapeño on a baking sheet and roast in the oven until the tomatillos are cooked through, 40–50 minutes—they'll be soft and slightly shriveled, and some of their juice will have sizzled out onto the pan.

Put the tomatillos and all of the juice you can scrape off the pan into a blender or food processor. If the jalapeño has blackened, rub the skin off with your fingers, then cut the pepper in half and remove the seeds (set them aside to spice up your salsa later).

Peel the garlic and add it and the jalapeño to the tomatillo. Pulse the blender or food processor until well combined. Taste the salsa and add as much of the cilantro, lime juice, and jalapeño seeds as you like, plus salt and pepper to taste. Give the mixture one more quick pulse to combine.

Store in a jar in your fridge to use every morning (and noon and night), the way we do. If you have more than you can use as a salsa, add it to a nearly finished braise to liven it up.

pickled red onions

yields 2 quarts

I learned about pickled red onions from the first cookbook that got me excited about food—Deborah Madison's *The Savory Way*. They are versatile, beautiful, and delicious, and they've been a staple of our kitchen since the first day. Place the onions in a glass jar with enough liquid to cover them and store in the refrigerator. Use them anytime you want a glimmer of color or bit of zing in a dish of eggs. They will keep for at least six months.

2 red large onions

5 cups boiling water

2 tsp kosher salt

1 tsp turbinado sugar

1 tsp black peppercorns, whole

1 clove garlic, lightly crushed

2 cups ice

3 cups white wine vinegar or apple cider vinegar

Trim the ends of the onions and peel away all the papery husks and tough outer skin. Keeping the onions whole, slice very thin (1/8–1/16 inch) on a mandoline or with a sharp knife.

Put sliced onions into a colander in the sink and pour the boiling water over them. Put the sliced onion, salt, sugar, peppercorns, and garlic into a bowl and lightly toss. Add the ice to the onions and pour vinegar over them.

pimento cheese

Bad pimento cheese was the childhood bane of most Southerners I know, but made with a little care, it's delicious. It's especially good on a hot biscuit, or grilled on a sandwich with country ham, or swirled into hot grits and served with sausage and broiled tomatoes.

2–3 red bell peppers

3/4 lb sharp cheddar, grated, at room temperature

2 oz cream cheese, room temperature

6 tbsp mayonnaise

2 tsp grated onion use a box grater or microplane and keep the onion juice

1/2 tsp cayenne pepper

1 tsp turbinado sugar

Roast the peppers by laying them directly on the flame of a gas stove, or by putting them under the broiler. Turn them frequently so that they blacken all over. Once they're almost entirely blackened, put them in a plastic bag or airtight container and close them in so that they steam. When they're cool enough to handle, peel off the blackened skins, cut out the stems, and open the peppers to remove the seeds and ribs. Cut them into thin (1/4-inch) strips, then cut the strips crosswise into 1/4-inch dice (yields about 1 cup).

Put all the other ingredients in a bowl or a standing mixer and beat until fairly smooth. When the mixture has made a coarse paste, add the roasted peppers and continue blending until they are evenly distributed.

hot sauce

yields 3 cups

This hot sauce was developed by one of the most energetic line cooks ever to work in our kitchen; it's a bright, spicy mixture that seems to capture his intensity perfectly. You can reduce the spiciness by removing some of the seeds and membranes from the jalapeños before you cook them.

1/2 lb jalapeños

1/4 lb tomatillos

8 cloves garlic

1 small onion

1 tsp kosher salt

1/4 cup apple cider vinegar

1/2 bunch scallion tops

handful cilantro

juice of 1 lime

Trim jalapeños by cutting off stems and removing some of the seeds and membrane to reduce spiciness. Remove husks from tomatillos and cut each in half. Slice onions and peel garlic and place into a pot with the jalapeños and 1 1/2–2 quarts of water, to just cover vegetables. Add salt and vinegar and bring to a boil over medium heat.

Cook for 40 minutes, or until everything is very soft, and remove from heat. Set aside to cool.

Pour the cooked mixture into a food processor with the scallion tops, cilantro, and lime juice, and process until everything is well puréed. Pour the sauce through a coarse strainer and refrigerate.

onion jam

yields 3 cups

This sweet and savory jam pairs well with roast meats. Onion jam and a few slices of seared duck breast on a piece of good toast make an excellent breakfast.

2 large yellow onions

2 cups apple cider vinegar

2 cups turbinado sugar

black pepper

Peel the onions, keeping them whole. Use a mandoline or a sharp knife and your best knife skills to cut them into thin slices. There should be about 8 full cups.

Put the rounds of sliced onion into a stainless or enamel pot with the vinegar and sugar—they should reach almost to the top of the pile of onions.

Add a pinch of crushed black pepper. Bring the onions to a low simmer over medium-low heat and cook until the vinegar reduces to about half and the onions have broken down somewhat—this should take about 45 minutes. When it's done the jam will be shiny and will seem a little loose—it'll firm up when you take it out the pan and let it cool.

Onion jam stores for up to a month in the refrigerator.

lemon vinaigrette

yields around 2/3 cup, good for a few salads

This is a simple but delicious vinaigrette, good for the farro salad (page 68) or for a bitter greens salad to go along with the fried oysters (page 135).

2 small shallots, minced

1 tbsp champagne vinegar

3 tbsp fresh lemon juice

drizzle of honey

pinch of kosher salt

1/3 cup extra-virgin olive oil

black pepper

a little fresh thyme or basil

Mix the shallots in a bowl with the vinegar, lemon juice, honey, and salt. Stir and let the mixture sit for 20–30 minutes. Slowly drizzle in the olive oil, whisking constantly to make an emulsified dressing. Mix in black pepper and herbs.

parsley sauce

yields 1 very full cup

This bright, herbal sauce gives a
heavy dish like steak and eggs a dash
of springtime lightness. You can add
or substitute different herbs for the
thyme, depending on what you have
available—try cilantro or celery leaf,
for example.

1 cup minced fresh parsley, leaves only

2 tbsp minced fresh thyme

2 cloves garlic, minced

3/4 cup olive oil

kosher salt

black pepper

pinch of red pepper flakes

2 tbsp lemon juice

Combine all ingredients in a bowl and mix well. Taste and adjust: It should
taste rich but bright, with a little heat but not overly spicy.

fig jam

Fresh figs were one of my mother's favorite summertime snacks—people at the beach we went to in North Carolina grew them alongside their beach houses, and my mother would sneak along the sides of their houses and snag fat, ripe figs from their trees and eat them on the spot. This jam uses dried figs, which I find at Sahadi's, a famous Middle Eastern market in Brooklyn—a far cry from the bright sands of Wrightsville Beach. The figs aren't much like the juicy ones my mother used to steal, but they make a nice jam that goes beautifully with cured country ham and aged cheese, as in our country ham biscuits (page 107).

yields 3 cups

1 lb dried figs

1/4 cup molasses

1/2 tsp kosher salt

1 tsp black pepper

1 1/2 tsp whole grain mustard

1 1/2 tsp white sugar

Cut the stems off the figs and discard.

Combine figs and all other ingredients in a saucepan, and stir well. Add water just to cover.

Bring the figs to a simmer over medium heat, then lower heat and cook slowly. Add water as necessary to keep the jam from sticking or burning. Cook until figs have broken down somewhat (an hour or so). Purée gently with an immersion blender or in a food processor, so that jam has a sticky but spreadable consistency.

Cool and store in the refrigerator for up to two weeks.

grapefruit vinaigrette

This is Egg's basic vinaigrette—it brings a bit of the breakfast palette into the mix with the reduced grapefruit juice. We use it most often in a simple salad of greens, roasted beets, and spiced pecans, but it goes well in a salad of greens, country ham, and deviled eggs, too.

yields 2 1/4 cups

1 cup fresh-squeezed grapefruit juice
any color will do, though pink juice makes a prettier dressing

1/4 cup apple cider vinegar

1 1/2 cup canola or grapeseed oil

kosher salt

black pepper

Pour the grapefruit juice through a mesh strainer to get the biggest pieces of pulp out. Transfer juice to a small sauce pot and bring to a boil. Reduce heat to medium-low and let the juice simmer until it's reduced by two-thirds and has a syrupy consistency, about 20 minutes. Allow to cool.

Put the reduced grapefruit juice into a medium-size bowl or into a blender jar. Add the vinegar and whisk or blend to combine. Slowly add the oil in a steady but slow stream as you run the blender, or whisk until the grapefruit juice, vinegar, and oil are emulsified. If the dressing starts to look thick before you've added all the oil, you don't have to use it all.

Taste the dressing and add salt and black pepper to taste. If the dressing is excessively sweet, add vinegar to balance it.

cucumber relish

This relish was inspired by a classic Southern side dish. Sliced cucumbers and onions in a light sugar and vinegar dressing made their way to our summertime table whenever we had ripe cucumbers in the garden. To be honest, I never liked them as a kid, but when I opened the restaurant, I saw that they could be employed to enliven some of our richer foods, like the fried oysters (page 135). As always, the better the cucumbers, the better your relish. Get them at a farmers' market at the height of summer or better yet, grow them yourself.

2 large cucumbers

2/3 cup water

1 cup apple cider vinegar

1 tbsp red pepper flakes

1 tbsp turbinado sugar

1 tsp crushed black peppercorns

1/2 tsp kosher salt

Slice the cucumbers in half lengthwise and scoop out the seeds with a spoon.

Slice the cucumbers crosswise in 1/8-inch half-moons.

Combine all the other ingredients—water, vinegar, and spices—in a bowl and stir until the sugar dissolves. Add the sliced cucumbers and allow to marinate for at least an hour before serving.

mustard-caraway vinaigrette

This is a pretty standard vinaigrette made a little more interesting by the simple addition of caraway seeds. This goes especially well with the smoked trout salad (page 137).

yields 1 2/3 cups

1 tsp grainy mustard

1 tsp ground caraway seeds

2 tsp chopped shallot

3 tbsp white wine vinegar

2 tsp honey

1/4–1/3 cup water

1/2 cup canola oil

1/2 cup + 1 tbsp olive oil

1/2 tsp minced thyme

1 tsp minced marjoram

1 tbsp minced parsley

2 tbsp minced green garlic, baby leek, or scallion
or a mix of all three

kosher salt

white pepper

Mix mustard, caraway seed, shallot, white wine vinegar, honey, and 1/4 cup of water in a blender. As soon as they come together and with the blender running, add the canola and olive oils in a slow but steady stream. If the dressing looks too thick, add a little more water and blend to loosen it up a bit.

Pour dressing into a bowl, add the fresh herbs and the minced garlic, leek, and scallion, and season with salt and white pepper to taste. Store sealed in the fridge until you need it. If the dressing separates, shake well to re-emulsify.

drinks

If you're like most people, the first thing you put in your mouth when you wake up is a drink: water, to counteract the dehydrating effects of sleep; juice, for quick sugar to energize you after an eight-hour fast; or coffee to compensate for the hour you spent tossing and turning instead of sleeping. And it may be that in your desperation you don't care much about how good your first cup of coffee or your first glass of juice is. But surely you should make sure your second is worth the trouble.

You can spend a lot of money on electronic coffee machines and juicers, but at Egg, we stick to the simple things: we make our coffee in a French press, or we let it steep undisturbed in water for 24 hours to make cold-brew iced coffee. For many years we squeezed all of our orange and grapefruit juice by hand in an old-fashioned lever-press, and that's still what I use at home. They're quiet, they get only the best parts of the juice, and they work when the power goes out.

Most days you don't want anything stronger than juice or coffee for breakfast, but on those special occasions you do, don't be hamstrung by convention. A Bloody Mary is a fine thing, but there's nothing wrong with having a straight beer or a glass of wine at breakfast. We like a light, spicy white beer, like Singlecut's Jan Olympic Lagrrr, or the excellent pilsner by our friends and neighbors at Brooklyn Brewery. Good breakfast wines need plenty of structure from acid or tannins, so we often pour a Muscadet or Txakoli if we want a white and a Cabernet Franc from Chinon or the Finger Lakes when we want a red. Of course, if you've got nothing planned for the rest of the day, go ahead and pour yourself a good full-bore cocktail alongside your breakfast hash.

bloody mary

makes 6 drinks

We spent a lot of time on our Bloody Mary recipe: We wanted one that tasted like a classic, with good tomato flavor and a broad range of spiciness—bright spice from horseradish and darker spice from dried chilies. Garnish your drink with a piece of celery or—better yet—a pickled ramp (page 169).

CHILE SPICE BLEND

3 ancho chilies

3 pasilla chilies

4 cloves garlic

1/2 tsp coriander seeds

1/3 stick cinnamon

2 tsp oregano

1/2 tsp ground black pepper

3 tbsp paprika

FOR THE MIX

3 cups tomato juice

1 1/2 tsp Worcestershire sauce

1 tsp chili spice blend or prepared chili pepper

1/2 tsp celery salt

1/2 tsp kosher salt

3/4 tsp hot sauce

1 tbsp prepared hot sauce

1/2 tsp black pepper

1/3 cup lemon juice, lime juice, or a combination

1 cup vodka

To make the spice blend, roast the garlic cloves and dried chilies in the oven at 350°F until the garlic is softened and the chilies are toasty and fragrant, about 15–20 minutes. Allow the chilies to cool. Remove their stems and seeds and then combine them with the garlic and all the other spices in a spice grinder or food processor. Pulse until powdered.

Combine all the ingredients except the vodka in a pitcher and allow them to sit for at least an hour or overnight.

To serve, fill a tall glass with ice, add a generous ounce of vodka, and top with the prepared mix.

mimosa

A simple breakfast classic, this has been the only cocktail we serve at Egg for years. The key to a good mimosa is good juice and good sparkling wine (Prosecco or Cava are the stand-bys, but a good sparkling Vouvray is eye-opening). You can punt and use cheap versions of both, but you'll taste the difference. Best of course is to squeeze your own juice, and since you're using a relatively small amount of it, it's not hard to do.

serves 1

2 1/2 oz orange or grapefruit juice

4 oz sparkling wine

Pour the sparkling wine into a glass and allow any bubbles to subside. Slowly pour in the juice. Allow the juice and wine to get to know one another for half a minute, then serve, with or without a twist of citrus rind.

cold-brew iced coffee

Cold-brew iced coffee is easy to make, but you have to wait a day for it to be ready. It's more delicious and less harsh than hot coffee that's been iced down, and a lot less trouble. We sell—and drink—gallons of it every day the temperature rises above 50°F outside.

serves 4–6

1/4 lb coarse-ground coffee

2 quarts water

Combine ground coffee and water and let sit in the refrigerator for 24 hours. Strain the brew through muslin or layers of cheesecloth. Serve over ice.

sweet tea

yields 2 quarts (8–10 glasses)

In the South, a pitcher of sweet tea in the refrigerator is an insurance policy against heat-induced misery. When the afternoon reaches its sultriest point, out come the ice-filled glasses, poured to the top with tea sweet enough to make your teeth buzz. It'll get you going in the morning, too—a fast and intense injection of sugar and caffeine that, like many a Southern host, won't take no for an answer.

8 bags black tea

2/3 cup white sugar

1 quart water

ice

Put tea bags and white sugar in a heat-proof container that can accommodate 2 quarts of liquid.

Boil 1 quart of water and pour over the tea and sugar combination. Stir briefly and allow to steep for 15 minutes. Discard teabags. Add enough ice to bring the level of the tea up to 2 quarts.

PRO TIP

Any black tea will do here. You can use something fancy, like English Breakfast, but the recipe will be just as good with Lipton. Frankly, the sugar will mute many of the subtleties of a fine tea.

winnie palmer

Here's a grown-up version of an Arnold Palmer, the classic combination of iced tea and lemonade. We named this drink for Arnold Palmer's wife, Winnie: Like her, this drink is big hearted and strong.

serves 1

2 1/4 oz bourbon

3/4 oz black tea syrup page 199

3/4 oz lemon juice

3 dashes Angostura bitters

6–8 leaves fresh mint, plus a sprig to garnish

Combine all ingredients but the garnish in a shaker and shake for 8–10 seconds. Strain into a Collins glass packed with ice cubes. Garnish with a mint leaf and serve with a straw.

new world bluff

Everyone knows sparkling wine is great for breakfast. But don't limit yourself to flutes of Champagne and mimosas: This tart and refreshing cocktail mixes sparkling wine with rum, bitters, and citrus juice.

serves 1

1 oz dark rum

1/2 oz lemon juice

1/2 oz grapefruit juice

1/2 oz cinnamon syrup page 199

2 dashes Angostura bitters

sparkling wine

orange twist

Put the rum, fruit juices, bitters, and syrup into a shaker with ice and shake lightly for just 3 seconds to chill the drink without diluting it. Strain the mixture into a chilled coupe glass. Top with sparkling wine and garnish with a twist of orange.

black tea syrup

Sweet tea is a staple beverage in the Southeast—it's what you drink to cool off until cocktail hour finally arrives and you can have something stronger. We sneak the flavor of afternoon tea in our cocktails with this syrup, which is the secret ingredient in our Winnie Palmer (page 198).

yields around 1 quart

4 tbsp loose black tea leaves
we use half Assam and half Russian Caravan

2 cups boiling water

2 cups turbinado sugar

peel of one well-washed lemon

1 oz vodka

In a quart jar, combine tea, lemon peel, and boiling water. Allow to seep for 5 minutes. Stir in sugar until dissolved. Allow syrup to sit until cool, then strain through a fine mesh to remove the tea and lemon peel. Add the vodka and refrigerate. Will keep indefinitely.

cinnamon syrup

For the New World Bluff (page 198), and a great thing to keep in your bar cabinet to add to any cocktail you wanted to give a warm, wintery kick to.

yields around 1 quart

5 cinnamon sticks

peel of 1/2 well-washed orange

2 cups turbinado sugar

1 pint boiling water

1 oz vodka

Break up the cinnamon sticks and add to a quart jar. Add the orange peel and the boiling water and allow to steep for 10 minutes before adding sugar. Stir until the sugar is dissolved, then let cool. Add the vodka and store. Will keep indefinitely.

fine, a smoothie

serves 1–2

I'm embarrassed to admit it, but I do love a good smoothie. After a hot run on a summer morning, it's a pretty nice way to refuel. This one requires bananas, which is one fruit we don't let through the front door of the restaurant. I keep them at home, though, and as they get very ripe I peel and slice them and throw them in a Ziploc bag in the freezer. Frozen bananas are the key to a successful smoothie, but slice them thinly—I've burned through a number of blenders by not slicing them thin enough.

1 ripe banana, thinly sliced and frozen

1/2 cup frozen blueberries

1/2 cup whole milk plain yogurt

1/2 cup orange juice

1 tbsp almond butter

1 tsp maple syrup

Place all ingredients in a strong blender. Run until smooth. Serve in a glass to drink or in a bowl with some granola on top.

Bryan Gardner and Heather Meldrom were a dream photo/food-styling team. They made making beautiful pictures a joy, never losing sight of the real thing. Thanks to Sacha Dunn and Matthew Axe for putting us in touch with them.

Caitlin Leffel, our editor, and Peter Ahlberg, our designer, kept this project on the rails in spite of my many efforts to steer it into a ditch.

Nick and Mary Lou Nahas, our neighbors in Oak Hill, loaned us props from their treasure trove of an antiques store, I. U. Tripp.

Melissa Vaughan and Irma Schreiber were thorough and patient recipe testers. Jenni Ferrari-Adler of Union Literary Agency kept me steady through the giddy process of signing a book deal.

I'd also like to thank the people who've made Egg a possibility, from Brian Benavidez and Melissa Locker, who gave Egg a place to incubate and inspired many of the decisions I made when we opened, to the incredible co-workers I've been blessed with over the years, including Maggie Nesciur, Holly Howard, Mike Porsche, Stephen Tanner, Millicent Souris, Ed Quish, Alan Berman, Charlotte Abbott, Krissy Viig, Eric Weaver, Maude Sernas, Michael O'Neill . . . the list could go on and on. Their fingerprints are all over this book.

Evan Hanczor, my co-conspirator, who came to Egg with no idea what he was getting into and has become a kind of third brother to me and the right arm I didn't know I was missing.

M'lou and Zettie, who have graduated from assistant butchers to perceptive critics and have tolerated more mornings and weekends without their father than I would like to count.

And, above all, Jennifer Tracy, who has been the single most important force behind Egg. She gave me the courage to start and the stamina to persevere.

First published in the United States in 2015 by
Rizzoli International Publications, Inc.
300 Park Avenue South
New York, NY 10010
www.rizzoliusa.com

© 2014 George Weld
Photographs by Bryan Gardner
Design by AHL&CO / Peter J. Ahlberg

ISBN: 978-0-8478-4483-8
Library of Congress Number: 2014952162
2018
10 9 8 7 6 5 4 3

Printed in China